No

Justice For

Bonnie

By Patty bickel

This is dedicated to my family that has gone through so much the last 25 years. May we all remember that we all have sought Justice for Bonnie.

I would like to thank my contributing editor, Jazmin Cybulski. My husband who always stayed beside me and my children who always contributed in ways they felt was best in seeking Justice for Bonnie. Also, my grand-daughter, Chloe Pasciuto, for assisting with the creative process for publication.

This has strengthened my testimony that there is a God who sent his son to pay for our sins and have that hope for an eternal life with him if we but repent and choose the right. He has given me the strength to carry on, search for the truth, and faith to move forward to help the cause and help others along the way.

Contents

1. Growing-Up ... 4
2. The Disappearance ... 11
3. The Investigation Begins ... 23
4. Lies and Deception ... 26
5. Differing Accounts ... 30
6. Where's Aaron's Home ... 34
7. Verbal Verbiage ... 37
8. One Year Later ... 40
9. Aaron's Care ... 44
10. Jeepers Creepers ... 50
11. Robbie ... 54
12. Two Years Later ... 56
13. Reinstatement Letter ... 60
14. More Deceptions and Lies ... 63
15. Fake News ... 66
16. No Justice for Bonnie ... 71

Chapter One

Growing-Up

Being a stay at home mom of six children may seem of little importance to the outside world; however, I enjoyed the experience. I volunteered at my children's school as a homeroom mother, a teacher assistant, a librarian, and a reading helper. I made many of my girl's dresses. I cooked most of our meals from scratch. I did all could to save money so I could stay at home to care for my children. I went through spinal meningitis, cornea transplant, bedwetting problems, grand mal seizures, broken arm, broken collar bone. It was hectic and frustrating time, but I would not have traded it for the world. Yes, it was all worth it. No, being a mother was not of great importance to me. It was a gift.

My husband spent 23 years serving in the U.S. Navy. Once he retired, he worked as a consulting engineer which took him all over the eastern and southern parts of the United States. This meant I was still the main parent in our children's lives, but that by no means meant my husband was an absentee father. He was there for us when we needed him for the better part of the time. His career meant our children were able to see the different parts of the country and experience different people and cultures otherwise unavailable to them.

Each of our children began their lives in their own special parts of the world. Liz and Veronica were born in Hawaii; Bonnie was born in Scotland; Michelle, and Robbie were born in Charleston, South Carolina; and Ginny was born in Norfolk, Virginia. As a family, we loved visiting the different museums, parks, and zoos wherever we were living. We played together, ate together, and prayed together. We even worked together.

When they turned eighteen, each child left to gain a higher education and work. As life sometimes goes, some of them had to come back home to live for a while. They were always welcome and they were always loved.

Bonnie loved to go over to Mike's house. Her friend Sandy lived a couple houses down from Mike's house and they lived three blocks from us. They all hung out together during their High School years, although, they did not go to the same schools. After Bonnie graduated from High School, she worked at a small business doing office work and accounting. She enjoyed the work. Bonnie and Mike married in 1987. I made Bonnie's wedding dress and flower arrangements and most of the food. It was lovely not elaborate but lovely. Everyone seemed to think so except for Annie, Mike's uncle's wife. She could not understand why I made Bonnie's wedding dress.

Mike was a co-owner of Harmon's Tool and Fastener. Berry Harmon was Mike's uncle who asked Mike to invest in the business with money Mike had saved. Mike was good at managing his money. He was a hard worker and liked to help his loved ones. He had a disabled sister that he helped take care of when his parents needed him. We thought Bonnie made a good choice for a husband.

Bonnie was a hard worker who knew how to save money. That is something that she and Mike seemed to have in common. I never heard Bonnie or Mike say a negative thing about anyone. They both seemed willing to help others without strings attached. Bonnie loved Christmas and to shop for the right gift for everyone.

When Bonnie and Mike started to look for a house to buy, they looked at a house two doors down from us. It had just been remodeled and had nice curb appeal. They looked at other houses in the area. Mike's aunt and uncle (Annie and

Berry Harmon) bought a home in the Orange Park area. Their old house about three miles away from us was for sale. They decided it would be great for Bonnie and Mike. They convinced them to buy their old home.

Bonnie worked at a computer store as an accountant. She liked working for the store; however, Annie Harmon, Mike's aunt, talked Bonnie into working for Harmon's Tool and Fastener. Since Mike was a co-owner of the business, Bonnie thought she made the right decision.

Bonnie was happy. Bonnie and Mike planned on taking care of his disabled sister, Stephanie, when his parents could not take care of her anymore. They took care of Stephanie when Mike's parents (Carolyn and John) needed time away or had a business function to attend. Bonnie and Mike had a plan to care for Stephanie when her parents could no longer care for her. Bonnie and Mike loved their family's and to have family get togethers at their home.

Bonnie became pregnant and had a beautiful baby boy on August 29, 1989. They named him Aaron. They seemed to be happy. Carolyn and John took care of Aaron most of the time when Bonnie and Mike went out by themselves or out of town. Then about year later things started to shift from Carolyn and John to Bob and me. I really did not spend too much time thinking about why. I knew or thought Bonnie still had a good relationship with Carolyn and John.

I did notice changes in Bonnie's behavior. She started to have her hair done at a salon along with finger nails and tanning. She was working and what she did with her money was her business. I knew she would not spend more than what she could afford.

One night about 11:30 pm after Bonnie, Mike, Annie, and Berry came back from a tool and fastener convention, Annie called to say she was afraid for Bonnie's safety. Apparently, Mike was upset about something, and Annie and Berry were afraid Mike would hurt Bonnie. Bob and I were surprised. We thought Bonnie and Mike had the same temperament as we had in our marriage. We did not yell or hurt one another when we had a disagreement. However, to reassure Annie as well as ourselves, we decided to go over to Bonnie and Mike's to make sure everything was okay.

When we arrived at their house, both Bonnie and Mike came to the door. They did not look distressed. There were no signs that Bonnie had been crying. Aaron was asleep. They both looked happy. When we explained why we came over, they told us that Mike was upset with Berry when he tried to get Mike to drink a bottle of this obnoxious mixture. I thought that was really sick. I figured Berry had to be a little on the drunk side. All seemed okay and they all worked together on Monday.

In May of 1992, Mike came over to talk to me. He was concerned about Bonnie being unhappy. She would not tell him why. I had the problem of not talking when something bothered me or I was depressed, however, it did not last for more than three days. Bonnie's had been going on for longer. She was not letting Aaron go over to Carolyn and John's place unless Mike took him over by himself. She was not inviting his family over for family functions. Mike even stated that Bonnie and her co-workers were sharing medicine at work. I asked if Annie knew this was going on and he said yes. I told Mike I would talk to Bonnie.

I talked to her a day or two later, but she wouldn't say much about her relationship with her in-laws. She dismissed the topic by telling me I "just didn't know the facts." When she and Mike dated for two years, she developed a good relationship with his parents. She trusted them to watch Aaron often. To turn on them so suddenly seemed odd. Bonnie also stated that she made her will and Liz, her oldest sister, would have custodial rights to Aaron.

I turned our conversation to the idea of taking prescription pills being passed around the office. I told Bonnie that if pills were being passed around at work that were not prescribed to the individuals, it could be physically and mentally damaging. I told her how I was worried about her sudden change in attitude. I suggested that if she were taking pills and stopped, she might see a change in her outlook on life and the people that really loved her.

Arron stayed at our house one week-end during the summer. A few days later, Bonnie called to ask if Aaron woke up screaming. I told he did but went right back to sleep. She was worried something was wrong because he had been waking up at nights screaming. I thought it was just missing his mom and dad. She decided to take him to the doctors. She told me that he may have worms. Her voice told me she was not convinced or she did not want to tell me what she thought the cause of the screaming episodes were from.

After a few months, Bonnie began to seem like her old self. She started to make her own clothes. She also began to include Mike's parents in family get togethers again. One such occasion was Aaron's third birthday party. Bonnie's family who were in the area were there. Bonnie invited Mike's family, which even included Berry and John's mother. Berry and Annie

did not get along with Berry and John's mother. Bonnie knew that but still invited her.

Everyone was enjoying celebrating our sweet Aaron when the joy suddenly came to a halt. Berry and Annie came bursting through the door. Upon spotting John, Carolynn, Berry's mother they announced if John, Carolyn, and his mother were staying, the two of them were leaving. Bonnie stated that they were staying. Berry and Annie handed over their gift for Aaron and left.

Though the relationship between Bonnie and her in-laws was mended, I would often be the one to pick Aaron up from his daycare after work or on my days off. When Bonnie picked him up from our house, we were able talk and she would share pictures taken of Aaron. I cherished that time together. She shared that she wished she and Mike would have bought a different house rather than getting sucked into buying Berry and Annie's old house. She wished instead that they had bought the house two doors down from us that went on the market around the same time as Berry and Annie's. She and Mike thought they were getting a good deal from Mike's Uncle and Aunt, she said "It wasn't such a good deal after all." When I asked her what she meant by that, she refused to elaborate.

Mike decided to do some remodeling to motivate Bonnie in doing something together. They made the spare bedroom into a place where they could do their favorite at home activities together. Mike had his work-out equipment, Bonnie had her sewing machine, and Aaron had his video's. It seemed a great plan for a young family.

Bonnie's crypticness continued into autumn. In September, she called to ask if I would babysit Aaron. This was a non-school day that I had off and had plans. I loved to help her out and take care of Aaron. I told her I would be happy to. Bonnie arrived around 8:30 am and she told me she was going to look for a new job. I was a little surprised, but excited for her. Around 10:00 am, Bonnie called to give me a heads-up if work called. She said to make sure not to tell them she was looking for a new job. I asked her if I should do the same if Mike asked. She laughed and said that he had helped write her resume.

Work never called and Bonnie came back around 3:00 pm. She was happy about her search, but also anxious. She wouldn't tell me why she was looking for another job. I was happy that Mike was supporting her and how she seemed to be back to her old self.

But then October came. Toward the end of the month, I was talking to Bonnie and she became hysterical. She kept going on and on about how she should have taken that job.

"What job?", I managed to get in.

"The job at the radio station off Dunn and Bush Drive", she said, her voice breaking. She confessed her hope that Memorial Hospital would accept her resume to work as a bookkeeper. She felt that the radio station might have been a job that lead to nowhere. But through tears, she would rather a dead-end job than continue to work at Harmon's Tool and Fastener. Again, she would not elaborate on why she was so upset about not changing jobs.

In November, Bonnie asked me if I would care for Aaron while she and Mike went to a Tool and Fastener conference in San Francisco, California. She said they would be going with Berry and Annie. I told her I would be delighted to spend the time with Aaron.

Aaron was a good child who was easy to care for. He did miss his mom and dad while they were away, but he was not overly fussy. As I was taking care of him, I needed something from his overnight bag, so I opened it up to get what I was looking for. Inside I noticed a letter. It was power of attorney forms addressed to me. To say this frazzled my nerves would be an understatement. I had never had the experience of holding such sobering responsibilities for Aaron or any of my other grandchildren, for that matter.

When Bonnie and Mike came home, they were giddy as teenagers. The exact opposite of what I had been feeling after finding those forms. They explained that during their trip Berry and Annie tried really hard to keep them apart. They were able to foil their attempts by sneaking off by themselves. I was glad to see them so happy.

That happiness did not last long. Bonnie called me a few days later and sounded really upset. She said she was hurt that I did not keep the power of attorney forms. I explained that I didn't know I was supposed to keep them. After my brief explanation, she completely shifted her tone and she said, "Oh, that's okay," completely shrugging away the previous dramatic, upset tone she had only seconds before.

Bonnie brought Aaron to the private school where her youngest sister, Ginny, was attending and I worked as an assistant teacher. She would even bring him to the school when we weren't there. She would tell me she did not want Aaron in Orange Park. She did not want him going to anywhere in Orange Park. Her sister Liz lived right at the border of Duval and Orange Park city limits. She stated she was not talking about Liz. That only left Berry and Annie. No other information would she release on the subject.

Bonnie started to establishing a new business for Berry in Granville, USA. She set a goal for it to be opened in February. I thought that would be good for Bonnie and Mike. I hated to see them move; however, it would get them away from whatever was going on at the Jacksonville office. Maybe give them more privacy to live their own life.

Bonnie came over one afternoon went into the room where Aaron slept and our other grandchildren slept when they stayed over. She sat on the bed, and said, "So, this is Aaron's room." That took me by surprise. I quickly stated that it was both his and my other grandchildren's room. "Oh, that's what I meant," she corrected in a strange sort of way.

The strangeness continued as Christmastime rolled around. Bonnie was not her usual self during Christmas. The excitement wasn't there nor was the time and effort at choosing Christmas presents. During a family get together, Bonnie and I were in the hallway outside the kitchen when she exclaimed, "I have some exciting news!" Listening in, her twin sisters shouted simultaneously, "You're pregnant!" Bonnie sheepishly said, "It isn't that. I want mom to watch Aaron when I go to our neighbor's funeral in Georgia." That was not what I would constitute as being "exciting news". Such an excited outburst for such a solemn occasion felt unsettling to my already building worry.

Bonnie also mentioned that they were scheduled to go to a conference on the 20th of January, but she did not want to go. She did not know whether Mike would be going. Again, she did not elaborate with any details.

The worry continued into January. On January 2, Mike pulled me aside to ask if Bonnie had confessed to me why she was so unhappy. He said he asked Bonnie if she wanted a divorce, and she really did not in the positive or negative manner. That was a shock to my system. I thought all of that was over. To me, it seemed life was beginning to move forward for them. I told him I would try to talk to her. I wanted to. I really did, but I never had the chance. Bonnie seem to avoid being alone with me. Since Bonnie had been going to Granville, Florida to set up the new Harmon's Tool and Fastener business, I saw this as a good, healthy movement forward. I figured she and Mike would move to Granville, get away from whatever was going on in the Jacksonville office, and things would get better for them. I thought her unhappiness would resolve itself and she and Mike would find happiness in their marriage again. But things just seemed to go backwards not forwards.

Chapter Two
The Disappearance

On January 7, 1993 Ginny and I got up and went to The Country School like we did every weekday. It was 10:00 am. I was in the middle of teaching math when I was called to the office. I was told I had a phone call which was highly unusual. I went to the office, picked up the phone, and It was Mike's voice on the other end. He explained that the police had him in for questioning. He told me Bonnie left home about 11:00 pm last night and had not come home, yet. He asked his mom to come and babysit while he went to look for Bonnie around 3:00 am. He asked if I had seen her, but I hadn't. It hadn't been 24 hours, yet.

It was difficult to understand that the police were already treating this as a murder investigation. Certainly, the police would call or come to the school to talk to me if they felt a crime had taken place or find out if I knew where she might have gone. Such a conclusion was so far beyond my imagination, I just couldn't process it. I thought she would be back any minute. Mike said he would call if she came back. Mike told the police that he and Bonnie had an argument before Bonnie left.

I later learned that Mike called in sick to work too that morning. Bonnie didn't show up at work. She didn't call. Determined to give Aaron a sense of normalcy, Mike or his mother took him to his daycare that morning.

But things were far from normal. The police officer who went to investigate searched through the purse and found that it belonged to Bonnie Harmon. He knew Berry Harmon and called Berry to—I assume—find out if he knew a Bonnie. From there, all hell broke loose. From that day on, my life was forever changed.

After his call, I waited on pins and needles all day to hear from Mike or the police. But no one called. When it was time for me to leave work, I had hope that nothing was wrong, everything had been resolved. On the way home, I told Ginny about Mike's telephone call. She said she had the same feeling as I felt, *this is not real*. If something disconcerting had happened, I thought we would most likely see a police car in our driveway once we got home.

There was no police car. At that point, I didn't know what to do or if I should do anything.

My friend Linda happened to be staying with us at the time. She and her husband were moving to Arizona and she was staying with us while her husband went ahead to begin his job and find a place to live. I decided to call my church leader to receive some advice on what to do. He told me I needed to call my husband. He said he saw on the news that Bonnie was missing and the police indicated that Mike had killed her. I felt sick. I told him that the police had not contacted me.

I called my husband, Bob, to relay what was happening. I could not believe that this was happening myself. I did not know whether he should come home or not. He was as confused as I was. He decided it would be best for him to take leave of absence and come home that next night Friday. I was relieved. I needed someone to talk to that knew all the people involved to see if this made any sense to him.

Linda said that she watched the news about Bonnie, and thought the description of Bonnie's car was the same car she thought was parked along the side of Duval Road on the way to the airport where she was working and at 5:00PM on the way home.

At 8:00 that evening who should show up at the door! Not the police. Annie Harmon. I did not want to talk to her. She went on about how she knew Mike had killed Bonnie. I did not say much in reply to her accusations or even recall all she said. She spoke as though she knew everything about Bonnie and Mike. She seemed far more on top of the situation than I felt I was. I wondered what I should be doing. I just felt like I could not act or react to something I couldn't believe was happening.

I called the school to tell them Ginny and I would not be coming in the next day. They were understanding and told me to take as much time off as I needed. They had watched the news and could not believe this was happening to me.

The next morning, Friday, Annie came to the door again. She nearly demanded that I get myself together and go to Aaron's daycare to pick him up. I was still in shock and couldn't process what she was saying. I wasn't thinking clearly, so I went along with what she directed. We went to Aaron's daycare.

When we arrived, the director of the daycare asked us to wait in her office while she went to locate Aaron. While she was gone, Annie decided to throw another punch to my gut by telling me Mike molested Aaron. When director came in, she trief to either soften the blow or to say that that was not a known fact about the abuse. Especially since they never reported any abuse. The daycare's director informed us that Aaron had not come to the daycare that day.

During our conversation, Annie's cell phone rang and she answered it. It was the police and they wanted us to go to Bonnie and Mike's house to pick Aaron up. I was feeling really disoriented. I wanted to go home, shut myself in and try to forget. If I did that, maybe this would all go away. But that wasn't going to happen. We were on our way to see Mike. The one who supposedly murdered my daughter and molested my grandson. All I wanted to do is scream, scream into a void all my anger, confusion, and frustration but that would have to wait.

We arrived at Bonnie and Mike's house to find no one home. I was relieved. Annie and I went across the street to the neighbor's house. This particular neighbor's husband had just died. It was the funeral Bonnie attended just a week earlier. The neighbor outside stayed with me while Annie used her phone inside the house to talk to the police. Her cell must have lost power. It was a very uncomfortable situation that crippled the two of us from talking. What were you supposed to say in an earth-shattering situation like this to a person whose husband just passed?

Annie came out of the house and broke the uncomfortable silence with an announcement that we would be going to Mike's parent's house. The police would meet us there with forms to take Aaron to the CPT Center (Child Protection Team) for Aaron to be questioned. I could not believe I had to endure going to Mike's parent's house. Supposedly, Carolyn and John helped Mike in some way to hide the crime. How could I go into their house and what do I say and how do I act?

I couldn't understand why I had to be there. I couldn't understand why the police were handling this in the way they were. Why hadn't the police talked to me before Annie? I thought things were as bad as they could be until we got to Mike's parent's house.

The house was dark when we were invited in. I was shown to the den and sat on the couch closest to the front door. Mike was holding Aaron across the room from me with his dad next to him. Aaron was not happy. He could probably sense that there was a problem, especially considering his mother was not around. I couldn't even go over to Aaron to say hi.

We couldn't even make small talk considering I could not comprehend Mike or his parents being a part of a crime let alone murder, and I imagine they did not know what I believed. The police came to the front door. They talked to Mike and Carolyn for a while and left. Annie came into the den and said it was time to go to the CPT Center. The police said it should only take 45 minutes. Annie still seemed to be in control instead of the police. Annie wanted me to sit in the back seat with Aaron. I knew I was in no shape to be near Aaron who may sense my nervousness. Aaron wanted to be near Mike's mom at this point. It was best for Aaron to be next to someone whose emotions were in better control at that moment than mine.

We arrived at the center around 10:00 or 10:30 am. Annie, Carolyn, Aaron and someone else went out of the entrance hall to another room. There were two officers, Detective Hickel and Morgan, in the entrance with me. It was at this moment seeing the police officers that everything hit me like a ton of bricks. This was real! I started crying uncontrollably. The detectives told me that I would have to get a grip. They wanted me to go in the room with Aaron while the CPT counselor questioned him. They needed me to be calm in order for that to happen. I went into the bathroom, blew my nose, willed myself to stop crying, and wiped my face with a wet paper towel.

I entered the room where Mike's mom was holding Aaron and the counselor were. Carolyn put Aaron down. Aaron came to me and sat on my lap. They did not want Mike's mom in the room since she may have been party to the crime and Aaron screamed with Annie around him. This left me in the awful position to help Aaron describe what happened the night before.

Aaron let me hold him. A young woman named Brenda asked many questions. Sometimes Aaron wouldn't respond, sometimes he'd look away, and sometimes he'd cry when she asked a question about Bonnie.

I finally could not take it any longer and started talking to Aaron about his favorite things or what he liked to do. Questions that I knew he could answer. Even with my efforts to get him comfortable, he still wouldn't comply with Brenda's questioning.

It was getting late. I was hungry. I knew Aaron was hungry and tired. But we endured all of this until around 1:00 when Aaron was finally asked what he would like to eat. He picked his favorite—McDonald's. Brenda left the room. It was about 2:00 when Aaron finally got his food. This relaxed him. He got off my lap and sat at a little picnic table to eat.

After he ate, we sat on the floor where some toys were organized. We played together for a few minutes when Brenda came back to the room. We played on the floor with Brenda for a while longer. Then, she started to ask questions again. Aaron remained relaxed and playful on the floor, so Brenda, Aaron and I stayed on the floor. He started answering the questions in a playful way. However, they may not have been truthful. They sounded to me like the imaginings of a three-year-old boy. I was not upset when Aaron said, "Daddy hit Mommy with the truck", or "her arm was bleeding". It sounded like play time with Mommy and Daddy.

Once I saw Aaron was okay, I got up slowly from the floor, I indicated that maybe I should leave at that point. Brenda shook her head yes.

I left the room and was greeted by a detective that seemed to be running the video camera. He comforted me and showed me the door to exit the room. I was hoping to get a drink or/and something to eat. When I entered the waiting room, it was obvious that that was not going to happen.

I found my way out and stood against a wall or a chair by myself. I did not know who to talk to or what to say to anyone. I felt better than when I arrived, but I still felt like I was in limbo.

Aaron's questioning was finished about twenty minutes later. We were all escorted to a small meeting room to decide who would care for Aaron while the investigation took place. At the end of the meeting at 6:00 pm, it was determined Aaron should stay with my oldest daughter Elizabeth. That was fine with me since I felt too confused about was happening and Liz seemed a neutral location for Aaron even though Mike and Mike's parents seem to be the best. I was far too confused and shocked to give Aaron the care he needed. He was familiar with his Aunt Liz and her two children were around his age. It seemed like a logical idea at the time, but maybe I was just too hungry, tired, and confused to think things through.

Bob arrived Friday night. I was a little tired and confused. We managed to get through the night. Not believing this was happening and, hoping Bonnie would get in contact with us.

The police were conducting a search for Bonnie on Saturday. Bob went on the search to try to find out information on what was happening. He determined that Berry was informing the police where to conduct the searches and finding no clues about Bonnie.

Bonnie's car was found in the long-term parking lot of the Jacksonville International Airport. That was surprising after a whole day to find it there. How, when, and why wasn't it located before then? The police had Michael watched, and he was with his father most of the time or with his lawyer. It seemed the first place to look and ask questions. Evidently the car was not there earlier. Someone gave them information about a car that fit the description of Bonnie's car with the emergency flashers flashing. Detective Hickel stated it was a hunch!

On Saturday, Annie stopped by our house and I met her in the driveway to let her know I didn't want to talk about finding Bonnie's body until a body was found. Without another word, she got in her vehicle and left. That would be last time we spoke.

Shortly after our last encounter, Annie had posters made to circulate throughout town. Though the poster had some informational mistakes, it was worth getting Bonnie's face out there the public's eye. This made me feel like I should be doing something more, but I didn't know what more I could do.

Friends came over to offer support in any way they could. Many men in the Church went on the search with the police but to no avail. The police searched Bonnie and Mike's house on Thursday and Friday using luminal (a substance used to detect traces of blood at crime scenes). They took objects from the house on the basis that they were "evidence". But all their efforts seemed of no use. We were no closer to finding Bonnie or what really transpired the last few months.

On Sunday, I stayed home from church. I just did not feel I could talk to anyone about was going on or connect with anyone. Later, Bob and I drove around to talk and think about what we knew about Bonnie, Mike and what was true or false about what was being stated so far in the search for Bonnie. We could not believe Mike would hurt Bonnie. We saw them as being similar to us. We really did not argue and fight. We usually had the same ideas or talked about the pros and cons of a situation before we made a decision. The more we drove the more we felt Bonnie was alive. We decided the best course of action was to meet with Mike. We sure didn't receive any information from the police, and it seemed we were receiving incorrect information from Annie and Berry.

Sunday evening, Detectives Hickel and Morgan came to our house. Hickel was the homicide detective and Morgan was the missing person detective. They asked for names of relatives whom Bonnie may have contacted, and they wanted our feelings on what happened to Bonnie. The latter seemed to be an afterthought.

Bob asked if Bonnie's car keys were in the car. The detectives said. "No". When asked if the keys were in her purse they refused to answer. When asked about the different prescriptive medicine of various types that had been found in her purse, the detectives said they had not determined what they were yet. As they were making their exit, they asked us to avoid contact with Mike and his parents.

    The detectives' advice had us a little bewildered, and what surprised us even more was the information that arose about Bonnie leaving Mike. She supposedly found an apartment in Orange Park, put a down payment on it, and was buying furniture for it. Mike supposedly found out about the apartment and that was what caused the argument on the night she left, Wednesday night. Upon investigating the situation, it was discovered that no new furniture was found. She had not given any furniture to friends or put in her house. It was reported that Bonnie and Annie contacted two apartment complexes in Orange Park the Saturday before Bonnie disappeared. One apartment that she put a security deposit on was picked up the next day. The second apartment was never identified and we could not find any information about it.

    The day that Bonnie and Annie went apartment hunting, Aaron was fishing with Mike. Considering the accusations of Aaron being abused by Mike, it seemed strange that Bonnie would leave Aaron alone with Mike. The story of her leaving them alone to go apartment hunting didn't seem like something Bonnie would do to me.

    Another accusation arose that Bonnie was looking for a daycare for Aaron in the Orange Park Area for Aaron to attend. Again, why would she look in Orange Park for a daycare for Aaron when she did not want him in the Orange Park area? She seemed as though she was considering The Little Country School where I worked.

We discovered that Bonnie picked up the security deposit the day after she put it down and had taken Aaron with her to relinquish the deposit. After doing so, she went to visit my mother in Palatka. The odd thing was that she only ever visited my mother when we had family get-togethers. Theirs was not the sort of relationship that meant casual drop in visits. When I heard about this visit, my immediate reaction was that this was probably Bonnie saying goodbye to her grandmother.

Detective Hickel called the house on Monday morning while Bob was handing posters out about Bonnie's disappearance. I told him things just did not add up, that someone was playing a game, and I did not like playing this game. He said he felt the same way and he was going to find out who was playing the game. At that moment, I had the strangest feeling he was part of the very game he claimed he wanted to end.

On Tuesday, January 12, the police, volunteers and Bob went to search different areas of town. Berry again selected the locations to be searched. After two days of that, the detectives decided the sites were speculative and a waste of time.

Against the detectives advise, Bob and I met with Mike and his dad on Wednesday, January 13, at our house. We learned that Annie and a Detective Jophur went to Aaron's daycare on the Thursday the very day Bonnie went missing to talk to Aaron and take him to the CPT Center. However, Annie's name was not on the list of people that could pick Aaron up from the daycare and Detective Noopur didn't have any forms that would enable him to take Aaron from the daycare, which is why Annie needed me to go with her to the daycare that Friday. Detective Jodhpur called the HRS 800 number to file a child abuse complaint. Annie was alone with Aaron asking him questions. Only Annie knows what she said and asked. Aaron was very upset and cried. It was unbelievable that the police would subject a three-year-old child to that kind of treatment the same day as the disappearance of his mother.

When Aaron was at the CPT building, he said "Daddy ran over Mommy with a truck". The police took Mike's work truck and found no traces of blood or damage. That was dismissed and the truck was given back. In a Christmas video, it shows Aaron was afraid of a new toy truck he received for a present. Mike and Bonnie played with it to show him it was just a toy and would not hurt him. It demonstrated that he was playing and remembered Christmas not what Daddy did to hurt Mommy. The rest of the interview with Aaron at the CPT was based on play time.

As time went on, information kept coming to us. During the time of our investigating, we learned that a Red Roof Inn maintenance man and a head maid noticed a man showing a lot of interest in the dumpster where Bonnie's purse was found. The suspicious man started watching from the balcony of the second floor then moved to within a few feet of the dumpster until the police came. To our disbelief, this information was not acted upon. The man was not found or questioned by the police.

Another interesting piece of information was Bonnie made a new will in November 1992 that changed the custodial rights of Aaron to me if anything should happen to her and Mike. That was a change in just a couple months. It did not disclaim Mike in any way as part of Aaron's life if she should die before he died.

Bob and I went to the apartment complex where Bonnie asked for her security deposit. The apartment manager suggested we have the Credit Bureau run a credit check on Bonnie. The Credit Bureau would not give us Bonnie's credit report. They did a check themselves and told us to have the police subpoena Bonnie's credit report. Detective Hickle said the Credit Bureau wanted a Grand Jury subpoena in order to do the search. To our knowledge, the subpoena never took place and the police were not giving us any information. We discovered that was false information about a grand jury subpoena.

John, Mike, Bob, and I made new posters to hand out and hang in various places with a two-thousand-dollar reward for information. We had the help of friends and family to hand them out. They asked permission to display the posters in various businesses in Jacksonville and surrounding towns. The police said it was normal for them to give a five-thousand-dollar reward for information. We decided we wanted people to contact us. This way, we might be able to find out information.

Despite their suspicions about Mike, the police didn't take Mike's guns from his house. There was no evidence that a gun was used in Bonnie's disappearance, but Mike's dad was afraid Mike might become depressed enough to take his own life. His dad decided to take actions into his own hands and gave Mike's guns to the police. The police kept them for a few days then gave them back. Mike and John asked if we could keep them. We put them in our attic. After two or three months, we gave them back. I am not sure where the guns went after that. Mike came to us a short time later to ask what happened to his hand gun. Since they were given to us in a gun bag, we weren't sure what could have happened to it. We didn't take an inventory before or after storing them.

Two weeks after Bonnie's disappearance, Mike and John came over with some prescription pill containers with various types of pills in them that Mike found under his and Bonnie's bed. We all thought it best to give them to the police to be annualized. When Bob and I confronted Detective Hickel for information regarding the pills, he said they were nothing. This was another item to add to the list of frustrations we had about the case and the police. We should have kept one container and had them analyzed for ourselves.

We received word that Bonnie and Mike's house was being searched again. This just hit me the wrong way. Why weren't the police looking at all the other evidence that seemed just as likely to producer answers to where and what happened to Bonnie. Bob and I went over to their house to see what was going on for ourselves. We arrived to see a few police cars in the yard. We asked what was going on and did not receive the right answer to my mind and I told them they were inept. I guess I was a little beside myself and Bob pulled me away but not too strongly. We had to leave.

With so many unanswered and ignored questions, we felt like we weren't getting anywhere. So, we decided we should hire a private detective agency to help investigate. We asked around about a good agency and called one we felt good about to make an appointment. Bob went on his own and decided to go with this one particular agency. They seemed to be reliable and knew how to obtain information that would help us find out what really happened in Bonnie's life before she disappeared.

After two weeks of being engrossed in the investigation, I decided I needed to work and Ginny needed to get into a regular routine. After a couple weeks of working, I had a parent come and tell me I needed to talk to one of their relatives about Bonnie. She worked at the Hertz car rental at the airport and had information about Bonnie. This parent was very adamant about this fact. This information took me by surprise and I didn't think to ask for name and phone number. I didn't see this parent for a couple of months. This parent was still adamant about me talking to her relative. I had sense enough to ask for a name and phone number of the relative who had the information.

My husband realized he needed to go back to work, turn in his termination papers, retrieve his 401K money, get his belongings and come back home to deal with this situation which did not look like a short duration. My husband's boss was very sympathetic. It didn't take but a few days for him to take care of the whole process. We were able to live off the 401K, his Navy retirement, and my pay for a year.

Meanwhile, the detective agency we hired found out some interesting information that indicated there were other people who were in the airport vicinity who claimed to have seen Bonnie with two other people the morning of her disappearance. This indicated she was still alive while police had Mike at the police station for questioning and before Bonnie's car was found in the airports long-term parking lot. Our detective agency was broken into and the agency was advised to stay off the case. They (we) were impeding the police investigation. The agency could not take losing their license. That was a big disappointment. However, they did continue to work with us.

Bob decided to use his own sources to do some detective work. He knew people connected to the FBI and other government agencies to help him. My husband thought about Bonnie and realized she would not stay at the Red Roof Inn where the purse was found. He decided to look at the Holiday Inn across the highway and about two blocks away from the Red Roof Inn. He found out a retired security guard had seen a woman that looked like Bonnie. He asked the motel if they kept records of the car tags and information on guests. They did; however, that would be something the police would have to retrieve. Bob was frustrated and disappointed that the police hadn't checked other hotels in the area and their records of guests during January 6th and 7th.

Amidst the disappointments, we gained some interesting insight about the possibilities of Bonnie's disappearance. I had a friend who worked for a doctor. She was discussing the case with the doctor when he said that it sounded like someone who wanted to completely leave the life she had and began a new one. I am not sure the police really pursued that line of thinking. When we brought it up, Detective Morgan claimed to have searched and found no evidence of Bonnie being at a shelter or seen as a homeless person. She still could have left town and started a new life.

I had Church friends that knew Annie growing up. They claimed she was a very controlling person who had to have the last word. One of my friends heard that one police officer that went to the Red Roof Inn and collected the purse was a friend of Berry's. He stated that Berry bragged about Bonnie being one of the office staff that was going to sue him for sexual harassment. Berry supposedly paid her $64,000 to be quiet and not sue.

That would have been unbelievable; however, my husband found that she did have a separate bank account that Mike knew nothing about. Mike did not know where the money came from or how much. They did their income taxes together and that money was not accounted for. All communication with the bank was addressed to Harmon's Tool and Fastener business on Runway Avenue. We also learned that Berry did have about three other girls from work that filed sexual harassment charges against him. The cases are public records which we have a copy of the case. One was a girl, K.J., who was very graphic about what would take place in the workplace some incidences occurred when Annie was present. K.J. won the case and was awarded a few thousand dollars. There were indications that the other girls dropped the charges because of threats of bodily harm made to them or their loved ones.

Also, public records show that Berry's last partner in business before Mike had a falling-out. Berry would not give the partner any money for his part in the business; whereas, the partner sued Berry for the money. Before the case ended, the partner dropped the case stating that Berry had threatened his family.

The cases show the integrity of Berry and Annie. How could the police stand behind them? How could they not look at the evidence presented that pointed to other than Mike? Wasn't it plausible that someone other than Mike wanted Bonnie out of the way? Perhaps for the protection of Aaron-- maybe even for the protection of Mike-- Bonnie saw the need for her to disappear.

A girl who worked for Berry stated that Bonnie, Annie, and Berry had a heated discussion in Annie's office about a second set of records that was not compiled by Bonnie who was the accountant. The girl stated that Bonnie was visibly upset during this encounter and even cried. Detective Hickel said that he conducted a search of Harmon's Tool and Fastener. They did not find anything amiss. It was noted that Berry and Annie were on the property at the time.

Children and Family Services (formerly HRS) conducted an investigation on Mike, Bob, and me. They found all three of us worthy to care for Aaron. On February 2, 1993, Aaron was returned to Mike. February 8, 1993 the HRS dropped their petition for Aaron's dependency. However, on February 10, 1993 when the organization, Guardian Ad Litem--who works closely with the police department--filed a petition for Aaron's dependency. The petition was amended for detention on February 12 and was granted by Judge Crenshaw on February 17.

Bob had a long conversation with Detective Hickel on February 20, 1993. Bob asked the reasoning for taking Aaron to the CPT. Detective Hickel said it was based on a hunch. The security guard at the Red Roof Inn claimed to have seen Bonnie. Detective Hickel said that the security guard was unreliable and "not playing with a full deck".

When Bob asked Detective Hickel if all the people registered at the Red Roof Inn were contacted, He said yes. However, the manager said the police asked only for a list of people who registered after 11 pm. Bob asked about Bonnie's purse and was told it was evidence but if there was anything specific Bob could ask. Bob asked if the medication had been analyzed. Detective Hickel said, "not yet". Bob asked if

Bonnie's keys were in her purse—that was confidential. The phone call produced no new information.

Our time was spent looking for clues to help us determine what happened to Bonnie and going to court about what was going to happen with Aaron. Nothing seemed to accomplish happiness for anyone. Aaron was now seeing a psychologist, Laura Creeper. Dr. Creeper had one agenda and that was to end visitation rights with all people who did not believe Mike killed Bonnie. Mike, his parents, and Bob and I lost visitation rights to see Aaron. The court had a "gag order" that stipulated that we could not disgust what was said or done in court to anyone.

On February 23, 1993, Bob talked to Special FBI Agent Thomas J Sopolewski for over an hour to determine if the FBI could intervene in everything that was going on. Agent Sopolewski said he would have to talk to his superiors and call back at the end of the week. An hour later, he called back saying there seemed to be no grounds for federal intervention. Agent Sopolewski said he had talked to Detective Ransom who said Bob was hampering the investigation and that Bob would not talk to the police without an attorney present. We did not have an attorney and Bob talked to Detective Hickel on the phone just a few days ago for an hour. We had a difficult time finding someone to help us fight our fight.

Bob decided to go to the state capitol to see if he could find out what to do about our situation by talking to Lucy Bartlett, Governors Aid for Citizen Affairs. She recommended that he talk to City Police Internal Affairs, get an attorney, file complaints against the city Sheriff and the State Attorney's Office. If we still were not satisfied, he could come back to discuss the situation with her. Bob informed her that Bonnie was missing and time was his enemy.

Through a friend of a friend, Bob was able to get an appointment with Gregory Smith the Governors Assistant General Counsel. He explained to Bob that the sheriff and state attorney are not "constitutional officers" and the state has no authority or control over them. The state department cannot oversee, critique, or criticize the way they conduct an investigation. He called Harry Shorts and asked him to talk to Bob.

Bob called Harry Shorts who told Bob to talk to the head of homicide Attorney George Batch. Bob called George Batch who told him to call a subordinate who was prosecuting the case. Bob informed him that there was no case to prosecute and no proven homicide. Bob told him that he would rather talk to him. So, George Batch setup an appointment. He called back a few hours later to cancel the appointment. He called Bob back a few days later. His reasoning to his department involvement in this situation was that the Sates Attorney Office has no control over the sheriff, HRS, or Guardian Ad Litem. Until the husband can convince Detective Hickel he is innocent, Mike will be the main suspect.

This was heart breaking to us to say the least. We couldn't understand why we had to go through such a difficult, long process, and everywhere we looked for answers, we seemed to hit a wall. We wanted to know why Aaron couldn't come home. We wanted to know what led to Bonnies disappearance.

Chapter Three

The Investigation Begins

We started writing letters. We wrote to representatives, congressmen, governors, the president, the sheriff, anyone and everyone. Some did not respond. Bob wrote to the ACLU stating that Bonnie's civil rights were being abused, as well as, ours. They would not take our case. Bob even wrote to agencies who helped pregnant women in troubled situations. They were polite but they found nothing to help us.

We even went to the Federal court house to give a letter to Bonnie if she was in the witness protection program. They accepted the letter with no guarantee it would be delivered. That seemed to backfire on us, because it was brought up in court, however nothing was determined from the fact that we did send a letter. We knew a friend that was connected to the FBI and he could not find any information that Bonnie was in the Federal Protection Program.

There were many court dates to gain back our rights to have visitation with Aaron even though he was living our oldest daughter. HRS was asked to have interviews with all parties connected to Aaron. All of the interviews from HRS stated that Mike, his parents, Bob, and I were suitable to care for Aaron. Each interviewer was removed from the case. HRS had no part in this case until the court brought them back a year later.

On March 17, the city police department received a search warrant on Bonnie and Mike's house, again. They searched inside and outside. They took carpet samples, took Mike's guns and ammunition, Bonnie's curlers and curling iron. They dug up a compost pile in the backyard. None of the search led to information or evidence as to what happened to Bonnie.

We finally had our visitation rights reinstated the end of March. It was so nice to see Aaron. He seemed happy during the visits. He seemed so happy to see his dad and the rest of us.

It was stated that Aaron told the psychologist that he was not happy and that his dad told him things that he was supposed to keep secret at the visitation center. The judge ruled that the visits be videoed. A camera was installed to monitor visits.

We kept receiving responses from government agencies stating that they do not have jurisdiction over local sheriff departments to investigate. The local agencies told us the same thing. We ran out of people to write to for help in finding out what to do to investigate our daughter's disappearance from all angles and not just Mike murdered her.

On April 17th, we were granted rights to have weekend visitation with Aaron. We had a nice time with Aaron over the first couple of weekends with Aaron. There were court dates to lengthen Aaron's visits with us due to Liz's change in working nights as a waitress leaving Aaron in the care of Liz's husband Dane. Her husband was not HRS certified to care for Aaron. There was mention in the latest motion that I questioned Aaron about his psychologist and tried to give him a negative feeling about her. This was untrue, but there was no way I could prove that I ever gave Aaron negative feelings about his feelings towards anyone. I would never make a problem worse for a small child to endure by giving negative statements about the tragic events of his short life.

Chapter Four

Lies and Deceptions

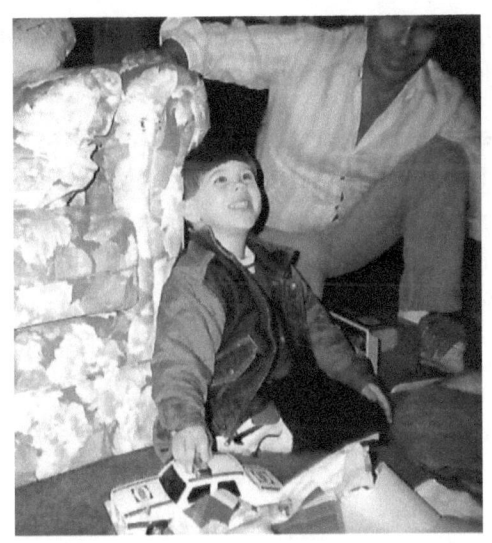

Bob and I had real issues with Detective Hickel. We communicated with Detective Morgan with the city police department missing persons department. However, there wasn't a whole lot he could do to help us. He had to go through his superiors on what to tell us and what he could do to move the investigation along. We did not gain information about the "evidence" we gave for police to investigate. We did not feel that we deserved to be lied to or about or have innuendos made that were never refuted that hindered our receiving custody of Aaron.

Detective Hickel at first said there was a tape of Aaron at the CPT that indicated Aaron witnessed that Mike killed Bonnie. From then on, he denied there was a tape. Detective work indicated there was a tape that was put in the State Attorney's office safe. He based his detective work on "hunches" rather than tips phoned into the police station. When Hickel was confronted with a lie, his excuse was, "that is a legitimate investigation technique to tell somebody something to see their reaction" or there was a misunderstanding. He was never able to produce evidence to back-up his hunches or investigation technique to qualify as positive resolute.

It took us what seemed forever to find a sketch artist to sketch a picture of a man that a security guard staying at the Holiday Inn in the vicinity of the airport the night of Bonnie's disappearance with Bonnie. The sketch artist who finally did the sketch was the son of a detective who took part in the investigation. Hickel said there was no sketch; however, Mike's lawyer asked for a copy of the sketch and was given one. The police continually said there was not a sketch and would not give it to the media. We did gain a sketch of the person. It did not help us make any connections after obtaining it.

Inuendoes were made in court about our credibility as parents when we were not present because we were going to be called as witnesses or when the party that supposedly made statements were not in court. We were not able to defend the remarks made especially when they were presented to the court through Hickel or GAL. The judge took their word as true without proof.

We lost our week-ends with Aaron because we allowed Mike to call and talk to Aaron on the phone. It was okay during a verbal statement in a court session when we asked about phone calls, but that changed when it wasn't stipulated in the court records. We were present during the phone calls. Aaron was very happy and no derogatory remarks were made. Aaron looked forward to his dad's calls before he went to bed at night which was 8:00 pm.

It was our opinion that Detective Hickel was spending too much time taking our rights as the victim's parents and our rights as grandparents away and not enough time finding what the evidence determined about our missing Bonnie. It took a toll on our emotions and what we could do to discover what happened to her.

We had many tips on people who may have seen Bonnie on the night or next morning of her disappearance. Some may have; others, we had to eliminate because of insufficient information.

At one point, we used a physic to help us determine where Bonnie might be. The police said he had helped them in the past. He led us to different parts of the state. We could not find any evidence to substantiate his findings. It seemed a way to keep us busy and out of harms way while the police could carry on with their agenda.

Our visits with Aaron were great. He was usually happy and energetic. He showed no signs of post-traumatic stress syndrome. One of the visits he had a sunburn. When we asked about it, he said he got it at Aunt Annie's beach house. It seems incredible that they should be able to see Aaron any time they wished, but we had to go through the court system to receive visitation time. What was more incredible was we were reprimanded for asking such a question.

Mike's attorney received an opportunity to present questions to the city police department and have the police give written answers to the questions. We were able to write questions we had and give them to Mike's attorney. This was in June of 1993. My husband gave Mike's attorney's office his list of questions. The questions stemmed from the same questions we had from the first couple months of our investigation.

- Names, addresses, and phone numbers of people at the Red Roof Inn that may have seen Bonnie on January $5^{th}/6^{th}$ 1993.
- Name, address, and phone number of man that the Red Roof Inn maintenance man said seemed to be watching the dumpster where Bonnie's purse was found.
- A copy of the Blanding Place lease application and receipt for deposit of the other place

> Bonnie made the Saturday before she disappeared.
> - The estimated time Bonnie's car was dropped off at the long-term parking area.
> - Inventory of contents of Bonnie's purse.
> - A copy of Bonnie's credit report?
> - Did Detective Hickle work in the Child Abuse Division previously?
> - Did Liz call on March 31st /April 1st about Aaron being sexually abused?
> - Did Hickle tell Liz to call and report it?
> - Has JSO subpoenaed Holiday Inn registration records for January 5th /6th?
> - Why wasn't the sketch of the man who may have been with Bonnie made public?

Mike's attorney later put all of them in question form and submitted them.

We still received tips from people who believed they saw Bonnie around the time she disappeared. Some, we told to call the police and report it to them. Others, we didn't feel they made much of a difference in time or date to substantiate Bonnie's whereabouts.

The home office of State Police Department made an appointment to see us in response to a letter my husband wrote. The meeting was helpful in finding out some information that the police would not tell us and we could not get through our investigators. They said they would check on details that the city police department were supposed to do in the first few months of Bonnie's disappearance. The city police department still denied there was a sketch of a man a security guard recognized as a man that was with Bonnie on January 5th/6th. The state police department showed us the sketch but could not give us a copy (which we later received). They also let Bob read the report on Blanding Place apartment.

Mike's mother, Carolyn, saw a girl that looked like Bonnie. She was able to write down the car tag number which was an out of state tag. We had it traced to a woman in a small town, on the edge of the state line to a trailer park that was owned by the Chief of Police. The woman looked a lot like Bonnie and the police said they would call us when they found out more information. If this woman was in any of the places that others said they saw Bonnie, we could update our data about sightings of Bonnie.

The city police did not call back. John went to the trailer park to investigate. The woman moved and left no forwarding address. The neighbors said she did look a lot like the phonographs of Bonnie. Sometimes it is two steps forward and three steps back.

We informed the police about Gail Bills. We also had our PI see what he could find out about Gail Bills. The PI had difficulty reaching her by phone. He went to her work place at Budget Rental and was told she was too busy to talk to him. The police told her she could not have seen Bonnie. In July 1993, Gail Bills told the PI that the police told her not to talk to us or our PI. Her relatives were still adamant about us talking to her. They were sure she had information that would help us find Bonnie or find out what happened to her.

Chapter Five
Differing Accounts

In August 1993, we found out that Gail Bills from Budget Rent A Car was told by police not to talk to us or our PI. That is why she would not respond to our calls or my letter. We were told that she saw Bonnie with an older woman and later they were gone and the emergency flashers were flashing on Bonnie's car. The information I received from the State Police Department report stated that Bonnie seemed greatly distressed.

The police turned over the requested answers to the questions Mike's attorney submitted. One of the questions requested information about the materials taken from Bonnie and Mike's house which stated that all of the material the police took from Bonnie and Mike's house for evidence did not show any demonstration of a crime scene. The Blanding Place apartment question showed that Bonnie did have a security deposit and an initial payment put down in cash with another $175 dollars to be paid later which meant that she was not putting in a new security system or buying furniture as stated by Annie and she picked up the security deposit the next day which indicated she didn't have plans on living there nor did she have time to think about a new security system or furniture.

I investigated many of the day cares in the Orange Park area that I thought Bonnie may have checked out. None of the day cares remembered the name or photograph. I was not too surprised in that finding.

The police document showed that Berry stated Bonnie was having an affair with a man from work by the name of Kurt Galleon. That man was interviewed and said the relationship began just a few weeks before Bonnie's disappearance. The police investigating the affair felt Kurt Galleon was truthful and did not have anything to do with Bonnie's disappearance. Kurt said he would take a polygraph test. The police document had a polygraph test. At first, the polygraph test looks as though it was done on Kurt Galleon; however, taking a closer look, the name on the polygraph is Curt Jellicoe. This was the name of the man that Sandy Wilden (a close friend of Bonnie's) said was Bonnie's boyfriend. He said in the polygraph test that he was Bonnie's boyfriend with about the same story as Kurt Galleon that the affair started a few weeks before Bonnie's disappearance. So, which one did Bonnie have the affair with or was she even having an affair?

There still seemed to be no evidence to show Mike hurt Bonnie or abused Bonnie to cause her to leave him. Mike had never been arrested. Yet, he was excluded from caring for Aaron, as well as, Carol, John, Bob and I. Hundreds, if not thousands, of letters were written by family and friends to the judge that stated that each one of us had good moral character to care for Aaron. Carol and John received a box full of letters stating that they were of good moral character to care for Aaron. The judge was not swayed by the letters. She gave the Harmon's and us each a box full of the letters and stated that there were many more. She also asked us to tell people to stop sending the letters that they would be thrown away unread.

The State Police Department let Bob see a copy of Bonnie's secret bank account. Bob was able to write down the information that was on the account. It was opened in April of 1990 with $375. It closed in August 1992. The check amounts varied and were less than what she opened the account with on the first bank deposit. They would not tell us who wrote the checks. We do not understand why she started the account, where the money came from, or why she closed the account when she did. This led to more questions than answers.

I am not sure anyone showed a picture of Bonnie to the bank personnel to establish that Bonnie was the actual person who opened the account and deposited the checks. It is difficult for me to believe she would have set-up an account with a bank that is in the opposite direction from work to home. Bonnie obeyed the law and did not cheat the government. The IRS taxes were completed jointly, and the money in the secret bank account was not accounted for on the tax statements. This would have been another reason Bonnie wanted to find another job if she found she had an account that she knew nothing about and closed the secret bank account when she found out about it a few months before she disappeared. This was information obtainable by the police not her parents. Was it obtained by the police—I think not!

The first part of September my husband met with Sandy Wilden who was a friend since high school of Bonnie's. She was one of the last people to see Bonnie. Sandy worked next to a Wal Mart in an eye glass store. Bonnie went to see Sandy after shopping the night of her disappearance. Sandy said Bonnie was looking for bar stools for the house (Bonnie and Mike's house) but could not find any she liked. Bonnie had given Sandy the last of the money that was in her secret bank account. Sandy gave that money to the police. The police did not give her a receipt until they were informed of their mistake. Sandy stated that she knew about the affair with a Curt Jellicoe who worked at Harmon's Tool and Fastener. Bonnie told her about the affair at the end of December. Sandy stated that Annie told her not to tell the police about the affair which she didn't until months later when the police questioned her about an affair. There has been no information on the police or anyone else interviewing Curt Jellicoe; however, the polygraph was given to Curt Jellicoe. That reaffirmed to us to wonder if there really was an affair.

The court session on the 10th of September 1993, clarified that Mike was not present at a birthday party for Aaron at Aaron's grandparent's house. This was important because people said that Mike was at the party therefore the grandparents went against a court order that he not be present. This court session also discussed what everyone should tell Aaron about his mother. We were reprimanded for telling Aaron we did not know where his mother was. Liz told Aaron his mother was in heaven. The judge ruled that it would be okay for us to say that we did not know where or what happened to his mother. CPT alleged that we should not have custody of Aaron because we did not believe Mike killed Bonnie. That seems a little contradictory.

In the next weeks court session, Annie stated that she went to the daycare on the 7th of January because the police asked her to and just to ask who brought him to the daycare, where his mother was, did he go for a ride with his dad last night, and did you go for a ride with mom last night. It is difficult to believe that the police would subject a three-year-old to those questions at such a difficult period of time. A three-year-old has no real knowledge of time frame. Last night could be a week ago. He obviously knew something was not right because his mother was not present that morning and those questions would have only disturb him more.

Annie also stated that I told her that I told Aaron we would eat and leave CPT to settle him down. I never talked to

Annie, and I did not say anything to Aaron about eating or anything else until we were in the interview room. How would she even know that when she was not present with Aaron and me at the CPT center. She stated that I left CPT hysterical. That is untrue. I was hysterical when I first arrived because I realized the unbelievable was really happening—Bonnie was missing and may have been murdered. The police could confirm what really happened because they were present when we arrived at the CPT Center.

Bob wrote letters in the hope of finding someone who would and could help us bring charges against the police and/or the psychologist in the handling of this case. No one was able to help us. Evidently, it was out of their jurisdiction or field of law. We continued to muddle through with the resources we had. We tried to be honest and straight forward and expected everyone else to be the same.

Mike's attorney, Tom Fallen had an assistant attorney, Eleni, who stated that she had seen a limousine at the federal court building with a girl that looked like Bonnie getting into it as they were leaving the court building. She wrote down the tag number-- EVE 94D. The city and state police said there was no such prefix. We kept looking at tag numbers. Bob found one with EVD from Pinellas county. The state police said that we misunderstood. It wasn't the EVE series that was never issued, it was the 94D that was never issued. We either wasted a great deal of time or we were being jerked around again. Shortly after this, Eleni was appointed to a judgeship. Did she deserve to be a judge? Yes. She met all the criteria. It seems many of the people in government type jobs or connections with this case that were genuinely supporting us were moved to other positions away from having connections with the case.

Chapter Six
Where's Aaron's Home

On the 6th of October 1993, Judge Pan's Order of Adjudication and Notice of Disposition Hearing was sent out. This order gives us information we did not know before or were not sure of until this time. Some information was different than what the police led others to believe.

The first fact stated was that Bonnie may not be dead; however, Mike was still blamed for her disappearance. There was no evidence to show she was dead. She had future plans that remained unfulfilled, as evidenced by the lease application she signed at Blanding Place Apartments, in which she listed herself as separated from her husband and noted that she would be living in the apartment with her son, Aaron, and as further evidenced by the quantity of money she had given to her friend, Sandy to hold which remains unclaimed.

The judges order gave leeway that something else may have happened to Bonnie other than that Mike killed Bonnie as the police were so adamant about proving. Bonnie gave every indication to me that she did not want Aaron in Orange Park where the Blanding Place Apartments is located and that seemed to be the only apartment complex mentioned indicating that Bonnie didn't demonstrate an interest in the other apartment complex. She went the next day to pick-up the security deposit at Blanding Place which indicates she didn't have that much of an interest in it either. Perhaps Annie was the one who wanted Bonnie to find an apartment.

Bonnie gave other indications she may be leaving by giving me Power of Attorney, closing the secret bank account, and accustoming Aaron to my workplace as his daycare. I was told that Bonnie gave Sandy the money for Sandy to save for Bonnie; however, I also was told she gave the money to Sandy for Sandy to keep. Bonnie had a large amount of cash in her purse. This gives an unclear picture of what really transpired the last few months of Bonnie's life before she disappeared.

The order said that her purse was undisturbed, that nothing was missing and that it still contained her credit cards and a large quantity of cash. I rather doubt that Mike would have left the cash and credit cards still in the purse. It would have been difficult to believe Bonnie would have left those in her purse, either. More questions without answers; however, it did answer our question of what was in her purse except what keys were in her purse.

Facts that were stated in this order about Aaron's statements to Ms. Meddlers and Dr. Laura Creeper months apart about his dad shooting his mom seemed to indicate to Judge Pan that Aaron did witness his dad hurting his mom; however, the order stated that Aaron also stated a few times in the past that his dad did not hurt his mom. The police were never to concerned about Mike's guns, and his guns were accounted for at the time of the disappearance.

The final part of Judge Pan's order was that Aaron became a dependent child in the temporary custody of our daughter Liz. Visitation rights would continue as adjudicated.

Bob and I decided to go over to Gail Bills unannounced to hear what she saw on the night of Bonnie's disappearance. We called our lawyer to see if she thought it would be okay to make the visit. We were told to go ahead. We pulled into her driveway to see a police car already there. We were asked to leave by one of the officers. He informed us that she did not want to talk to us because our people harassed her. I do not know what people harassed her, but it was not us. I would not have even thought about going to her house, but her relatives kept saying we needed to talk to her. I decided to write her a letter stating we just wanted to find out what happened to our daughter. The letter was never answered. That was my last hope to find out directly from her what she saw.

Chapter Seven
Verbal Verbiage

A court hearing on the 5th of November raised many upsetting moments for us. Laura Creeper seemed to think that anytime we said anything about Bonnie to answer Aaron's concerns were wrong and that it interfered with her therapy. We had not been given a clear answer as to what to say and what not to say. Now, it was questioned about telling him to pray for his mom. The "remember when" game to remember good times was also not a good thing to do with Aaron. As a general rule, we did not bring up the subject of his mother unless he did.

We had always had clothes, books, and toys at our home for Aaron. That did not seem to be right. Evidently, Aaron did not have enough at Liz's home. We were told we spoiled Aaron by giving him too much of everything. We are that way with all of our grandchildren except for Liz's because of visitation rights. We felt (feel) that it is part of being grandparents. We get to spoil our grandchildren.

When Aaron came to the visitation center with bruises, bites or sunburn, we would ask him about them. Sometimes, just to have something to talk about. This was wrong according to the supervisors. We were pumping him for information that did not concern us. It was more difficult to find something to do and talk about with Aaron after each hearing.

We were told we defended Mike even though the "evidence" shows he killed our daughter. We have never defended Mike. He has a lawyer. We were defending ourselves trying to reach the truth and find out what happened to our daughter. We continued to ask for "evidence" that indicated our daughter was dead and that Mike killed her. Never were we given any "evidence".

Bob and I were tired of the negative views we were given by Laura Creeper, GAL, and the police. We could not do anything that pleased them. What they wanted is to have our rights as grandparents taken away from us unless we condemned Mike. Denise Waterpool an attorney for GAL once laughed in my face and said they could keep Aaron from us until he was eighteen. Did we really deserve that type of reaction?

Court dates seem to be on for every other week or asked for a continuance. That means more money for lawyers and time away from work, family, and trying to figure out where or what to do next.

The court had a gag order on this case from the beginning that limited us from talking about the case to just about anyone. In December, the gag order was clarified by stating that normal media investigation could go on not prohibiting free speech. The gag order was just for court proceedings. That was still very limiting because most of our complaints were through court proceedings that had misleading information and statements even when we were not present.

Christmas was not going to be the same. We had to wait to go through court to decide if, when, and how we were to celebrate Christmas with Aaron. On the 14th of December, Judge Pate found that we could all have Aaron for a few hours. Carol and John had Aaron on the 24th, and on the 25th Liz brought Aaron, Katie, and Kyle for a few hours to our house. It was strained but at least we saw them for a short time.

The court order came out on the 30th of December that Liz would still have temporary custody of Aaron with visitation rights for grandparents and Mike. Mike would see Aaron on supervised visits at the visitation center. Carol and John would have Aaron on the first weekend of each month. We would have Aaron on the third weekend of each month. We were not to bring up the subject of his mother. If Aaron brought up the subject, we were to reply in a neutral manner. What a neutral manner was, we had not a clue nor did they seem to have a solid meaning.

Chapter Eight

One Year Later

It was one year from the time of Bonnie's disappearance. It seemed a much longer time with nothing to show to help solve what happened and why. Liz, Annie, and police wanted a memorial service for Bonnie. They received permission to have one at the City International Airport. Liz organized the service. The newspaper contacted us. We were not interested in having a memorial service since we felt Bonnie was still alive.

Channel 17 had a news story on the one-year disappearance of Bonnie. They did not show the sketch of the man who seem to have an interest on what was going on with Bonnie's purse that was found in a dumpster nor did they telecast Bob and me. Liz was the one that was shown, and she violated the gag order around 17 times. We are glad she did not get in trouble for it, but it was aggravating how law enforcement and people who believed Bonnie was murdered by Mike did not have to abide by the same rules ordered by the court.

We were receiving phone calls from people who had a missing relative and wanted our help. There was not too much we could really hep them with. We did not seem to be able to help ourselves. We really felt helpless. We learned about some cases that the police had their minds made up like the city police department and they could not move forward, either. There were people that called who had relatives who were arrested for a crime they didn't do or a relative was murdered and they could not get the police to investigate other than who they felt did it. In one way, it was comforting to know that we were not alone in our pursuit of justice.

The story hit the news again for a memorial service that was to be held at the cities international trade port near where her purse was found. Liz organized the service. Bob and I thought it was inappropriate since we still believed she was alive. There was no evidence of a murder or a body. Again, we were left out of the process. The rest of the family that was in town and my mother were in attendance. We felt a little betrayed, but still held on to family values and their differing opinions. The article did mention that Mike and his family were not present. Of course, he would not be there if he did not believe she was dead for the same reason we were not there.

Bob noticed another poster of a missing woman. Tonya Perry who was 22 years old, 5'4" tall, brown hair, brown eyes. She disappeared October 12, 1993. We wondered if there could be a connection. We could not see any real evidence that they were connected. Of course, the police did not see a connection.

A friend called and told us a psychic said to look for Bonnie at the end of Pace Road near a construction site near an old dump. Bonnie is in the middle of three dirt piles he stated. Bob looked on Pace Road. There was no construction, no old dump, and no three dirt piles. No Bonnie.

Bob was offered a job at River Bend. We were beginning to feel the pressure of needing money to pay for attorneys, PI, and living expenses. It met back on the road again for Bob but that was where the money was at and finding clues, leads, and information about Bonnie was not coming forth. I think he was really tired of trying to get information and receiving none. Plus, the roadblocks and "misunderstandings" by the police.

Troubles really began to come into Liz's life. She was having trouble holding jobs due to court sessions, therapy sessions, and now a divorce from her husband. Another place for Aaron to live needed to be decided. Linda from HRS Protective Service asked Dr. Laura Creeper to meet with me to validate Aaron living with us. Dr. Creeper's letter states:

As you know, I have worked with Aaron in therapy since February 18, 1993. During this time, Aaron has lived with his aunt, Liz. Ms. Liz is no longer able to care for Aaron at this time due to the overwhelming effect Aaron has had on her household, particularly her two young children. Since Aaron has had weekend visitation with his grandparents, his behavior has been particularly disruptive. He reports to Liz that he does not have to mind her, that she is bad and that he doesn't have to share with the children. It appears that Aaron has been given this message while on his visitation with his grandparents (this was a ludicrous statement. I nor the Harmon's would ever say such things to upset Aaron or make him feel unloved by those around him.)

As you know, at the court hearing regarding custody and visitation it was my recommendation that Aaron have no contact with his father or either sets of grandparents. None of these family members were able to be supportive of Aaron's disclosure that he witnessed his father (or "the monster that lives inside my dad") shoot his mother. It is my opinion that Aaron's continued exposure to nonsupportive family members has resulted in his being unwilling to disclose further details about the murder, or about his previous report that he was sexually abused by this "monster". Although it is clear by observing Aaron's play that both the shooting and the sexual abuse are present in his thoughts and continue to cause him anxiety, he has systematically refused to actively discuss either topic in therapy. It is essential to Aaron's recovery that he be able to discuss these events and his feelings about them.

Because Mrs. Liz is no longer able to care for Aaron, a new placement must be found. I requested that I meet with the maternal grandparents to determine whether or not they would be able to be supportive of Aaron's disclosure. Mr. Pasciuto was unable to come in to meet with me, so I met with Mrs. Pasciuto in my office this morning. I was encouraged by Mrs. Pasciuto's openness in discussing her feelings as well as my past conclusions and recommendations in this case. However, because I was not given the opportunity to talk with Mr. Pasciuto, it is impossible for me to make a recommendation regarding Aaron's placement in their home or to be able to change my recommendations regarding contact with the grandparents. I would be glad to meet with Mr. Pasciuto in the future and make further recommendations at that time.

If you have questions regarding this case, please contact me.

End of letter.

Our attorney wrote back asking that to move this forward if she would consent to a telephone conference with Bob. She would not do a telephone conference nor is she in her office on Monday or Fridays the days Bob could meet with her without too much of a problem with his work assignment.

As to Laura Creeper's letter, there has never been any statements made that the police found evidence that a shooting took place that killed Bonnie. Quite the opposite, they seemed to rule out a shooting took place. The sexual abuse was labeled unfounded by doctors and other professional people. We have always showed our support in our daughter Liz's care for Aaron. We would have been glad to meet with Dr. Creeper, but it was obvious she did not want to meet with us.

Chapter Nine

Aaron's Care

The detention hearing was set for March 7th. That court hearing stated that Liz was the one that recommended us to take care of Aaron. That disagrees with what Dr. Laura Creeper said Liz was saying about us. HRS Protective Services found no reason for unsuitability for us to be Aaron's caregivers.

The GAL had objections to our being the caregivers. They were not ready for this hearing and it was not an emergency to them. CPT objected because we did not believe Mike killed Bonnie. HRS said it was a semi emergency since current placement was not working and Aaron was regressing. So much for being innocent until proving guilty!

Judge ruled that Dr. Creeper interview Bob ASAP, and we should refrain talking to Aaron about his mom. Another hearing set for April 3rd. The interim placement would be Laura Creepers call.

Bob met with Dr. Creeper on the 9th of March. Laura Creeper stated that she understood Bob to be of good character and had Aaron's best interest in mind. She consented for us to care for Aaron, continue Aaron's visits to her, and not talk to Aaron about his mother unless he talks about her, and then we were to listen, make notes, and give the notes to her.

On the 16th of March, 1994, we were given temporary custody of Aaron. We were to have no contact with any of the Harmon's, we were to take Aaron for his visits to see Dr. Creeper, take him to the visitation center for visits with the Harmon's, and have open contact with Liz and Dane.

Soon after we received temporary custody of Aaron, Kathy Sins, our attorney, said that in good faith we should drop our appeal to gain custody of Aaron. That sounded reasonable to us and she used to work for the GAL. We went ahead and the appeal was declared moot. We should have realized by now that that was really a bad decision considering the lengths taken to take away our parental rights.

All seemed great. Aaron came and the first thing he said is, "They said I would be here forever." I was afraid to question him. I wondered who told him that and felt apprehension about the future. Aaron was happy and adjusted fast to the routine of getting up going to school with Ginny and me, and going to his class. I stayed a short time in his class each day until he adjusted to his new environment. It did not take more than a few days for him to adjust. We would all go home together, eat, play, get ready for bed, which was 8:00, then Aaron would wait for his dad to call. We had a verbal okay for the phone calls that had not been written in the court records (another mistake we made). He was always waiting happily for the phone calls from his dad. We would be right there and never heard anything that would upset or suggest a negative feeling towards anyone from Mike. Aaron went right to sleep each night after the phone call. We went back to court where Liz did state that she heard in court that the phone calls were acceptable. The court said we had to stop the phone calls. Aaron was not happy about not getting to talk to his dad before he went to sleep, but he just seemed to deal with changes as they came.

The police, Laura Creeper and GAL did not want Aaron in our home. They seemed determined to find something to convince the court to place him in foster care. How would that help Aaron adjust to life without his mother or father?

On the 13th of April, the judge put Aaron in foster care. This court date was just supposed to be about visitation rights of John and Carolyn's. This was a shock for everyone. What was this going to do to Aaron? He has had so many changes in the past year. Why was this happening?

Again, the findings were based on lies and innuendos. The phone calls from Mike to Aaron were determined appropriate verbally in court. The HRS knew that our son was arrested a few times and knew he was not violent just a teenager who made wrong choices. They determined that Robbie's being in our home was not a problem. Robbie lived with Liz and Dane for a while Aaron was living with them and that was perfectly okay. Now, the court said he was violent, charged with armed robbery and stole guns which were stored on our property, and we knew it. He was never arrested for armed robbery, dealing in stolen guns, and no guns were found on our property. The police did come out to our home twice looking for guns late at night. Supposedly, another teenager had turned Robbie in for a plea deal. They never found guns or any stolen material. Our son stayed at our home for a short while (less than three weeks) then moved in with friends.

The day HRS came and picked Aaron up was devastating. I held it together until he was put in the car and then I became hysterical. I could not believe anyone could do this to a family without due process. We were guilty of nothing and an innocent child was being abused by the "system" that was supposed to protect children.

On the 21st of April, there was a court hearing to see if another adult relative could have custody of Aaron. Berry and Annie Harmon entered their interest in taking on that role. They showed good cause for this alternative placement. They had a beautiful home, owned their own business which had a value of four million dollars stated in the petition for custodial care by Berry Harmon. We put in a motion to reinstate our appeal for custodial rights. Carol and John filed for their visitation rights. It just seemed to be a vicious cycle.

May 6,1994 the Judge ordered in the negative for all parties. If Liz and Dane could not resume custodianship of Aaron he would go into foster care. Again, the negatives were very biased for Mike, Carol, John, Bob, and me. It was unfair to Aaron to deprive him of the relatives who had loved and cared for him for the first three years of his life. The ones Bonnie wanted Aaron to continue to love and care for him that was stated in her will and the power of attorney papers.

Our contact with Aaron would be through an HRS counselor. We could ask her questions about Aaron and give things to Aaron through her. I was supposed to believe and trust a system who had tried to alienate our family members for the past year and a half. I could not continue to deal with this type of contact. I would rather talk to relatives of ours or Carolyn and John Harmon. I just felt void of feelings. We could never say or do anything right.

On the 17th of May, Cyn D, from GAL, gave a sixteen-page report on a background to continue the course of action to keep Aaron away from paternal, maternal grandparents, and Mike. The report did say on page 12 that if Aaron requests it or demonstrates that he misses his father or grandparents than visitation would be considered. Another, yea right when hell freezes.

May 20, (Bonnie's birthday) 1994 the Judge put out an order making us non-parties which meant we had no interest or part of Aaron's custody battle. Laura Creeper wrote a statement that locked the doors to any further action on our part.

Dr. Creeper stated that Aaron, a four-year-old child, voiced his belief that Mr. and Mrs. Pasciuto did not support his statement that he saw his father kill his mother and called his dad the monster that hurt his mom. She stated that Aaron had no desire to visit with us. She went on to state that Aaron was doing so much better with no visitation with Mike, his parents, Bob, and me. Aaron's behavior was supposedly aggressive and secretive during the period visitations took place and after the visits stopped, he was a model child.

This was not the behavior we saw when he was at our house or the visitation center. Aaron did not seem traumatized. He was very loving and happy to see us. He never seemed secretive or aggressive. While he was with us, he accepted change without demonstrating negative feelings that caused problems in his behavior or at school. This is not the picture that Liz painted of life at her home with Aaron. Liz's children told us that Aaron said he loved us without us asking any questions about Aaron. It is impossible for me to believe that Aaron never talked about us and that the anxiety that he demonstrated was more from not being with the people he spent most of his life with rather than because we did not believe something he may or may not have witnessed. I was a special education teacher for many years and worked with children who were abused, saw a parent killed, and had been taken from that environment into foster care. I saw first hand how they reacted when taken from their family such as it was and they were very aggressive and difficult to work with in a classroom. They always choose to be with their family no matter how terrible it was.

It is also difficult for me to believe that a three or four-year-old child would say that he does not believe or we do not support him when he says the monster hurt his mom. At different times the monster has been different people. We had never talked to Aaron about what happened to his mother, and he never talked to us about what happened to her. Since Ms. Creeper did not have a video tape of Aaron saying or even demonstrating that his father killed his mother, it has been very difficult to believe this actually happened.

The order went on to state that Bob was in contempt of court and could be jailed for not complying to a court order. This order was to reveal the location of Bonnie which he suggested that he had information where she may be. They decided not to arrest my husband since we were ruled as non-parties. However, they postponed the contempt charges to May 27th. Just more harassment. My husband did have information on where Bonnie might be if she was in a protection custody program.

Dr. Creeper wanted to discontinue videotaping Aaron's therapy sessions. She did not feel that it was necessary. The judge did rule that the videotaping should continue since her office was setup to do the videotaping. However, it was mentioned that Dr. K, Mike's therapist for Aaron, told Aaron that he had been videotaped and if he would like to see himself. This evidently changed Aaron's view of the therapy sessions. The judge changed her mind when she found that out without asking Dr. K why he said that and ordered that the videotaping stop.

On the 27th of May the contempt charges were dropped. Bob did have a press release ready to give to the press. The press did not come to the court house. The gag order was still in effect so they were not allowed in the court room, or the police told the press that it was not happening so there was no need for press to come. The press release was so well written as to what we were going through I am stating it:

A year and a half ago I would not have believed that I would find myself in this position. For months I was quick to tell anyone who would listen of every piece of information I had found. Then I realized that "the authorities" were not following up on leads identified, but they were actively suppressing information and isolating me from opportunities to search for my daughter. Police officials have recorded conversations, ordered people not to talk to me or my private investigator, an attempted to justify their actions, threatening to jail me and my private investigator.

Unless every lead is followed up thoroughly instead of suppressed, it will jeopardize the conviction of anyone the police attempt to charge in relation with my daughter's disappearance. I do not wish for an innocent person to be convicted, nor do I wish for a guilty person to be acquitted due to police errors of omission and commission.

The night security guard at the motel where my daughter's purse was found claims to have seen my daughter. The police have decided to discredit his testimony by describing the security guard as "not playing with a full deck", and "intimidated" by family members who questioned him. Neither characterization is reassuring about a security guard.

The motel maintenance man identified a person who seemed very interested in the dumpster. This person was later picked up in another Florida city for stalking a school teacher. When this person failed a polygraph test, city police department was notified. The city police department responded that the person should be released, "they have the husband".

A motel maid who claims to have seen my daughter was questioned several times by the city and state police department without weakening her conviction as to what she saw. She was finally able to sit with a sketch artist who produced a sketch of a man allegedly accompanying my daughter. The city police department has not only failed to release the sketch but have denied its existence.

An airport car rental employee who claims to have seen my daughter and a companion was ordered by the police not to talk to me, my wife, or my private investigator. When my wife and I arrived at this person's home, the police officers were there, and my wife and I were asked to leave.

In my opinion, the authorities have tried to discredit every witness that I identified to them. The authorities have ordered witnesses to be silent.

I want to find my daughter. "The authorities" will not help me and have hampered my efforts in the past. I will continue to search for my daughter until I find her. I will not allow the authorities to handicap my efforts any farther.

If there are people out there who have information whether or not they have given it to the police, I ask that they give that information to my attorney, Kathy Sins, or our private investigative agency. We will act on that information and maintain confidentiality.

Like many Americans, I have lost a lot of the faith in and respect for "the system". Judge C has elected to take this personally and find me in contempt of her court. (She did choose not to find my husband in contempt.)

I feel that she is just adding insult to the injury and losses that I have sustained in the last 18 months.

End of press release.

This press release expresses what we had gone through without seeing any progress in finding our daughter. We had to deal with not only the loss of our daughter but the loss of her son, our grandson. Words cannot express how we felt and there seemed nothing we could do about the injustice that had been served us.

Chapter Ten

Jeepers Creepers

It was a struggle to find a way to appeal since we were non-parties. We decided to go to a Church counselor. We were impressed with Dr. Copes. She could not believe that a therapist would declare visits with immediate family was damaging to a young child, which she viewed as quite the opposite. Dr. K, Aaron's second therapist, viewed Aaron's symptoms were due to being taken from his family. I would think that two out of three therapists would show the court that another look at the situation would be advisable.

The GAL, police, and Ms. Creeper had other plans. The first course of action was to have *Unsolved Mysteries* do a program about the disappearance of Bonnie by having an interview with Mike. When Mike was contacted, my husband wrote to *Unsolved Mysteries* to let them know a few things about the case. *Unsolved Mysteries* wanted the interview with Mike. If no interview with Mike, no television show about Bonnie's disappearance. No television show took place.

Next came motions from HRS about Bonnie leaving without taking Aaron or making any contact with Aaron for over a year which made her an unfit parent and if she did not complete a performance plan it would terminate her paternal rights. It completely contradicted her being dead. This seemed ludicrous to me. Yet, it was another step to show cause for Aaron to be placed in foster care.

For the next few months, it seemed letters and motions were remitted to have us reinstated as a party to gain visitation rights and to have Aaron viewed by another psychologist who would also view Laura Creeper during a therapy session with Aaron as she shows him individual photos of Bob and me that she requested. That did not please Dr. Creeper. The therapists, Dr. Creeper, K, and Copes, were to make ground rules for us when we have visitation with Aaron. The ground rules seemed to be a difficult matter to be established because it dealt with what is said to Aaron about his mother and getting all three therapists together to make the ground rules.

The foster parent, Ms. Frans, made a report of events of what Aaron said or demonstrated over the next few months. One statement he made was that he forgot to tell them he wanted to see his dad. An hour later after he said that he wanted to see his dad, he piled pillows in front of the door to keep everyone in and they couldn't get out. A week after that he told Ms. Frans his dad stuck his finger in his butt and that dad is the monster. After saying that, she stated that Aaron started to cry uncontrollably. I would like to know what transpired before this happened and who he was calling dad at that time. It is a completely different Aaron than I ever witnessed.

Ms. Frans' report sounds very incriminating towards Mike. However, when you think "about the facts", such as Aaron was actually two when the finger in the butt took place and he was five when he made the statement to Ms. Frans. That abuse stuff was unfounded by several professionals. It is a bit unbelievable that a child of two would remember a happening that was reported unfounded. A child of two has usually had poopy diapers or underwear that his bottom needed to be cleaned. In the past, Aaron has stated that many different people were the monster, and he has had different "dads" the last few years. It is my opinion that others would have to keep bringing the subjects up about the monster and sticking a finger up his butt for him to remember such an event. While he stayed in our home before and after Bonnie disappeared, Aaron never said or demonstrated any type of abuse. He had never shown any type of discomfort towards Mike. It was quite the opposite.

Another document that was submitted by HRS on a home study of my daughter Veronica and her husband Jeff that was very bias and gave false information about our family. The reason it gave for doing the study was that Aaron was placed in foster care since "the family was in a big war over the child." That was never an issue. Different members of the family who were capable to care for Aaron submitted forms after Liz was unable to continue caring for him so he would be taken care by a member of the family.

The document went on to state other "facts" about Veronica and our relationship with her that was untrue. It stated that we visited her a few weeks earlier which was a highly unusual event. My husband visited often to help Veronica and her family with various projects at least once a month if not more often. It stated that we did not know about her decision to care for Aaron. We may not have known the initial decision to do so, but it was soon afterward, and we were pleased with her decision. Our daughter Michelle and her husband also submitted forms to care for Aaron. Our other two children were not of an age and responsibility to submit forms. There was no war of any type ever in our family even when our opinions differed.

There were other bias opinions in the report, however, the stated areas were the ones that are the most demeaning statements about the family. The quoted quote at the beginning of the document suggested to the HRS interviewer that the family was at war over who would/should care for Aaron. An example of the punishment I used on her was misleading. Veronica said that I spanked or used time-out. Veronica stated that she could not remember being spanked. When asked about her dad, Veronica stated that he thumped her on the head and she didn't like that. It seemed that if a statement was negative about Bob, the interviewer made the statement appear almost abusive. The interviewer was interested in knowing if Bob sexually abused Bonnie and if Mike had a hold on us because of he knew of the abuse. This is not the first time this has come up about my husband abusing Bonnie. It stems from Detective Hickle and his method of investigating. Veronica did not understand what that had to do with her caring for Aaron.

The interviewer hadn't informed Veronica that she was coming. Her husband just came back from being deployed over-seas and she was overwhelmed with the unannounced visit. Veronica was not confident that she had a chance to gain custodial rights because of her family's finances at that time. She just wanted the family to know she would like to help in any way she could. That interview nearly pushed her over the top. She wanted to be home to help and know what was happening concerning Bonnie and the rest of the family which was not possible.

The phycologists were all able to meet and determine ground rules for the grandparents to gain visitation rights with Aaron. The grandparents gained visitation rights in December 1994. However, on the 15th of December the city police department and the State Attorney's Office objected to the visitation plans and wanted the visits to be suspended for four weeks. Our visitations seemed positive. Carol and John's attorney said that a decision needed to be made in four weeks not a discussion. Judge C would be assigned to another court division and Judge H would make the decisions.

Our visits with Aaron went well. We were able to give him the designated Christmas presents. He was still easy to please and a happy-go-lucky child and seemed pleased with the Christmas presents. There wasn't much communication between the Hamon's and us. We did not know the reason behind city police department and the State Attorney's office to stop the Harmon's visits with Aaron. We were glad we were still able to continue our visits with Aaron.

During these last few months, Bob was driving back and forth to his job in Baton Rouge, home, and Texas. He did not want to miss an opportunity to visit with Aaron, and he enjoyed helping Veronica and her children in Texas. He had been doing this for a few years. His health was still good but it was taxing on him. There were times when the visitation times were scheduled that Bob was not able to make arrangements to the visitation center to see Aaron. It was difficult for me to understand why we needed visitation rights. We still had a child in our home and raised five other children.

Chapter Eleven

Robbie

On December 14, 1994 Robbie was arrested. He and his girl friend Janet, who later became his wife, were out driving around a not so nice part of town when Janet had an anxiety attack and wanted out of his car. Finally, Robbie let her out. He thought if he drove around the block she would get back in the car. She didn't want to. Someone saw what they thought was not right and called the police. The police arrived, handcuffed Robbie, and put him in the back of the patrol car. We are not sure what the police were doing or how much they talked to Janet. We do know that two officers were standing by the patrol car saying things about my integrity. Robbie asked them several times to stop talking about me. He could not take it any longer and kicked out the patrol window. The officers reacted immediately by dragging him feet first out of the patrol car, ground his face in the glass from the patrol car window, while Janet yelled that he was an epileptic. They called an emergency vehicle. Robbie was in surgery for seven to nine hours that included having a plastic surgeon come in to put his face back together without damaging his eye.

Surely the police could have talked to Janet and realize that there was no harm to her by Robbie and that he was not violet, talked to both of them, give them a warning, and let them go home.

In the police report, there was no explanation of how Robbie received the injuries or the seriousness of the injuries. They ended up putting Robbie on a work release program. It caused Robbie to be labeled a felon. There is no place on his records where he was connected to using a gun or dealing in stolen guns.

Robbie was able to go to ITT Tech and received honors in the computer programming field. He latter went on to become a master mechanic where he worked mainly on the heavy-duty vehicles and equipment as well as the computer work that goes along with the job. He did not find work in the computer programing field because of his felony record.

Robbie had always gone out of his way to help those around him. It did not matter the shade of their skin or the sexual orientation of that person. He helped them because it was the right thing to do. He was not a violent person; however, his seizures were violent to his body and mine. There were some people that made fun of him because of his seizures. He did not let that get him down.

He passed away the Saturday after Mother's Day in 2017. His medication finally did its damage along with energy drinks to keep him awake to manage three jobs to pay for medicine, insurance, and paying for his student loan. A month after paying off his student loan he had a heart attack at work.

Just as every aspect of Bonnie's disappearance, the police had unjustifiably judged our family.

Chapter Twelve
Two Years Later

At the second-year anniversary of Bonnie's disappearance, Detective Hickel and McMann stated on the TV news that they were close to an arrest. They mentioned items such as Aaron was an eye witness, a shoe print in Bonnie's car, the apartment Bonnie had, and the secret bank account. Nothing new was stated and all items were not enough to make an arrest for two years. Mike was not arrested nor was anyone else.

On January 12th, a "discussion" in Judge H's chambers with the different attorneys involved in this case minus Mike's and our attorneys'. Since it was to discuss the visitation rights of the paternal grandparents, Mike and his attorney were not present and our attorney didn't see the need for her or our need to be present either. That was a mistake of our attorney and our part.

It was a 38-page discussion that consisted of arguments from the police attorney, GAL attorney, CPT attorney, Aaron's GAL attorney who seemed to be there on behalf of Laura Creeper on one side and Carol and John's attorney on the other side. That did not seem to be a balance in pros and cons of visitation rights being granted. The reason for the discussion and why some attorneys and Mike and our presence were not there was clearly stated.

At the beginning of the discussion, Ms. Waterpool, the CPT attorney, stated that Bonnie was deceased which was corrected by Carol and John's attorney to missing and the police stated that Mike is responsible for her disappearance. The discussion turned to the orders of Judge C. on visitation procedures. At times, both sets of grandparents had visitation rights. Then, visitation rights were discontinued between both sets, and then just the maternal grandparents had visitation rights. During this part of the discussion, Laura Creeper's reasoning for not wanting the grandparents to have visitation privileges was stated that Aaron's progress in therapy was regressing. Dr. Copes' name was stated as having a difference of opinion from that of Laura Creeper's, however, that did not seem to have an affect on Judge H. Since we nor our attorney were present, Dr. Copes' agreement with Dr. K was not stated.

It was noted by Mr. Kow, the police attorney, that the discussion was just for the visitation rights for the paternal grandparents. Carol and John's attorney discussed the facts that there were no allegations brought against Carol and John in the two years of this case. She brought up the fact that we lost visitation rights for a time because we did not believe Mike killed Bonnie. Mr. Kow stated that the police felt that the Harmon's visitations could harm Aaron psychologically.

Mr. Wein, Aaron's GAL appointed attorney, began his discussion on how well Aaron's therapy was going without any grandparents' visitations. When the maternal grandparent visits started, Aaron's progress regressed. Opps, he said maternal grandparents and this was about paternal grandparents. Then he stated that "We say it is not possible to specifically relate Aaron's regression to the visit with the maternal grandparents, but that certainly was a possibility." He went on to say it could be just the holidays not being the same as in the past. He said that the paternal visits would be detrimental to Aaron psychologically as stated by Mr. Kow.

Mr. Wein stated that Laura Creeper's opinion was that if the visitations resumed it could hurt Aaron's mental health. She would not stop the visits indefinitely but would stop them until she felt Aaron was ready psychologically.

The judge restated what the doctor said that therapy regressed when maternal visitations took place. The discussion went back and forth about visitations and the courts order for discussion was on the paternal visits. Ms. Waterpool brought up the fact that Dr. Creeper said it would be best if no visitations would be best at this time due to the psychological damage that might take place because of suppressed memories of his mother's disappearance. Aaron did so well in therapy when there was no visitation permitted. Aaron was helping in the investigation during this time of no visitation.

Ms. Butter, the Harmon's attorney, brought up the fact that Dr. Creeper's statements of what Aaron said and her notes did not coincide. Dr. K's opinion did not agree with Dr. Creeper's. Ms. Butter asked for video tapes be made of Aaron's therapy sessions to collaborate what Aaron was saying and how he was saying the things about his mother and father. She tried to persuade the judge to see that Aaron was so close to his grandparents that it may be detrimental to Aaron's mental health.

Mr. Kow and Ms. Waterpool would not relent on how well Aaron's therapy went when there was no visitation by the father and the two sets of grandparents. They would not state what Aaron was saying that was showing progress because of the sensitivity of the case. Dr. Creeper's therapy room was not equipped to use videotaping. This did not leave Ms. Butter any defense for her clients nor us. There was no mention of our therapist since our attorney and we were not present.

Different discussions about in-camera hearings with Aaron and Dr. Creeper were discussed. It seemed that the in-camera hearing would be with Dr. Creeper and Judge H would decide whether visitations would take place and when. The in-camera hearing would not be released until or if there is an appeal. This led to Judge H stating visitations between Aaron and maternal grandparents would end until he ruled that visitations would resume.

This was another time when our attorney and we were not present to defend our rights and good name. Another time we were dismissed as not being an interest or relative to the case. Again, there seemed to be a case building on statements a three/four-year old may have made that would culminate in the arrest of his father but has never came to that. If the statements Aaron made were so sensitive and important to discovering what happened to Bonnie, why hadn't that evidence been enough to arrest Mike? It was enough to take visitation rights away from Aaron's closest relatives but not to accomplish peace of mind for anyone as to what happened to Bonnie and a proper placement for Aaron.

Bob came late to the "discussion" and the bailiff would not let him enter the judges conference room. He tried to explain but the bailiff would not let him into the room. Ms. Sins asked for a rehearing on the matter since she nor we were present to discuss our reasons for continued visitation. Judge H set the hearing for March 29, 1995-two months away.

Ms. Sins talked to Judge H. who was apologetic for the bailiff not allowing him into the conference room. He also said that even if Bob were there, he would have made the same decision. He felt that scheduled meetings between the different parties of lawyers, Detective Hickel, and us would be beneficial to resolve some of the issues.

Meetings were set-up, however, Bob and I had difficulty in meeting with Detective Hickel who we could not believe and Mr. Wein who we felt was working more for Ms. Creeper than for Aaron's best interest. We did not feel the meetings would dissolve any issues. We would need goals and objectives set for the meetings.

Bob reminded Ms. Sins that Judge H had asked Mr. Kow if the police had the affidavit of diligent search and Mr. Kow said no. The police did not subpoena Holiday Inn Registration, the Barnett Bank for the records to identify the source of the checks to Bonnie. There was no collection of the mail to her work address. There was no search of her work site in Granville that she had recently set-up before she disappeared.

The first meeting with Detective Hickel, Laura Creeper, and attorneys amounted to nothing. No real information and no tapes or videos to indicate what Aaron really said about his mother or what may have happened with real evidence to prove what he said happened. There was no blood found inside or outside of Bonnie and Michael's house to indicate a murder had taken place. No evidence that a gun was ever used around that house. No evidence that Aaron was awake at that time especially since he was usually asleep by 8:30.

The second meeting was similar. We were told we just needed to believe what Aaron said without being negative. We really never had the chance to hear Aaron talk about his mother. His teachers all said he was a bright sweet child. That was before and after Bonnie's disappearance. Not usually the way children react to seeing their mother murdered. We were told we needed therapy other than Dr. Copes.

Chapter Thirteen
Reinstatement Letter

We wrote a letter stating why we should have visitation reinstated:

March 29, 1995

BACKGROUND AND REASON FOR GRANDPARENTS RIGHTS TO BE REINSTATED:

On January 6, 1993, our daughter, Bonnie, disappeared. We really did not know what to think at the time. The police did not contact us until three days later, even though they had felt Bonnie had been murdered soon after her purse was found in the dumpster early on the morning of the 7th. We could not believe that the story was on the television stations before we were even aware something may have happened to her.

I, Mrs. Pasciuto, was told on the 8th that Aaron may have been abused by his father. At that time, Mrs. John Harmon, Annie Harmon, and I took Aaron the Child Crisis Center. HRS wanted Aaron to be taken from his father's custody. I felt that Aaron would be better in his aunt's care until we were able to find out just what happened. No one assumed it would take long to find answers.

We did not intend for our rights as parents and grandparents to be taken from us or put in such little or no regard at all. Aaron was in our home so often for the first three years of his life. I just had the bedroom that Aaron slept in redecorated before Bonnie disappeared. Bonnie's commit was "I like Aaron's room". She knew that our other grandchildren slept there, too, but Aaron was the one who stayed with us the most.

When Aaron was in our care from March 6, 1994 to April 13, 1994, he was so happy and "normal" we thought we would be able to get our family's life back to pretty much what it had been. Aaron was greatly traumatized when he was taken away. If the school he attended at that time was asked how he was doing, they would tell you that he was a wonderful student, eager to learn and who got along well with the other children.

We have been told so often throughout the last two years how happy and normal Aaron is, except at court hearings. That is very difficult for us to believe they are talking about the same child. I have been around all different kinds and types of abused children. I do know how they act and react to the different abuses. I also know that they don't care to talk about the abuse over and over again. Many children will tell you that they want to forget about it and just be loved and respected for who they are—A Child of God.

We have no problem dealing with Bonnie's death, if she is in fact dead. That would be easier for us to deal with than what we have gone through this past two years. If there were any evidence to support that a violent act took place at Aaron's house or with one of their vehicles, that would have given it support. I had a doctor tell me before he knew Bonnie was my daughter, that leaving your purse and even children you loved behind is not uncommon but common.

For the past year, we have been concentrating on gaining custody of our grandson. We feel the police did not do what they should have done to thoroughly investigate our daughter's disappearance but, our real concern is that of our grandson. He is five and a half now, it won't be long before other children ask him about his family and grandparents. I have taken care of children for almost forty years now. I know as children grow older thy want to know more about their family and need to know why or why not they are loved by that family. I believe it is time that Aaron knows he has a family and is loved by that family, no matter what has happened. The Guardian Ad Litem and The Child Protection Team say that Aaron may not tell us what he saw. They are afraid we would not believe him. Whatever happens, I can assure you, we would never tell or indicate we did not believe him. We want Aaron to have a completely full and normal happy life. We have always abided by the court orders.

Respectfully submitted,

Chapter Fourteen
More Deceptions and Lies

Ms. Sins then gave us a copy of the HRS report sent to Judge H. The report supports the fact that Mike completed all that was expected of him to regain custody of Aaron in September 29, 1995. It states that Aaron has always socialized well with his peers and enjoys interacting during play activities. Aaron was in the Gifted Program at the age of five. That indicates he was well adjusted. Where is the evidence of regression?

The report stated that reunification goal was set for June 19, 1996. Later in the report it stated that the reunification date was March 19, 1996. Yet, Mike has not seen or talked to Aaron in over a year due to a stated fear he has of his dad that manifested months after the disappearance when he had no contact with his dad.

That report ended our chances for an appeal or any other contact with Aaron. When we visited Liz, Katie and Kyle let us know that Aaron misses us. We told them that we missed him too. That was the end of the subject. How ironic when we were told that he never mentioned us and if Aaron indicated that he missed us "they" would begin visitation again, he supposedly told Laura Creeper and his foster parents he didn't want to see us.

We told our attorney, Kathy Sins, to send us her final bill. We felt she lost our right to appeal and did not defend us as grandparents. We lost our daughter and now our grandson. Where was the justice!?

To add insult to injury, by the 26 of January 1995 Bonnie was to have completed a psychological evaluation, parenting skill classes, proof she can provide for her child's financial needs, sign an information release, and explain her absence to the court. Obviously, she did not complete the plan. This gave them reason to terminate her parental rights without an attorney to speak in her defense. Nor did we have an opportunity to give a statement in her defense.

The next foreseeable event was to have Mike's parental rights taken away to pave the way for Aaron to be adoptable. That seemed to be unobtainable since Mike had not been arrested for any crimes and no evidence to indicate he had murdered our daughter.

On April 19, 1995, Judge H made the following *factual* findings:

1. The child firmly believes and reports that he saw his father kill his mother, <u>and that another family member helped.</u>
2. The child says that his father has told him that he would kill him if he tells.
3. The child fears contact with his father, and even the prospect of same is sufficient to cause him great anxiety.
4. The child believes that his <u>paternal</u> grandparents, the child fears that they too will put him at risk of seeing his father, which puts him at great risk of being exposed to his father; and as for the <u>maternal</u> grandparents, the child fears that they too will put him at risk of seeing his father.
5. The child has exhibited a rather clear pattern of behavior, which supports the Court's conclusion here. During those periods when he has been exposed to his father or grandparents, he suffers from anxiety, enuresis, and aggressive behavior, and regresses in his therapy. (Footnoted that this led to the child's aunt

deciding to give up custody of him.) On the other hand, during periods of no contact with family members, the child's symptoms lessen, and he makes progress in therapy.

What drivel! How could that be the same child that was cheerful, interacted with his classmates, and was an A+ student? How could that be the same child who could not wait for phone calls from his dad and not have any problems in our home with anxiety or enuresis when he had visits with his dad and paternal grandparents? The footnoted statement that that is the reason why Liz gave up custody is ridiculous. It had been stated by the same court that I had been the reason for Liz's divorce. Mike, his parents, and we were unable to defend ourselves against the accusations made from a judge who took over this case after a year and a half had gone by.

Now, the unobtainable seemed to be in reach. There was no evidence to the accusations made either in written statements during a therapy session, no videotaping of the therapy sessions, and no collaboration with a neutral party such as school teacher or psychologist to confirm Aarons supposed anxiety episodes. Yet, the findings impacted a whole family unit. How did this bring justice to the disappearance of Bonnie or peace in the life of a small child?

Chapter Fifteen
Fake News

This was not the end. We hadn't given up on finding out what happened to Bonnie or being reunited with Aaron.

We wrote letters to representatives, every new mayor and sheriff, and every new governor in the state of Florida. We still tried to use the influence of our friends and relatives to find clues or information to help us locate where Bonnie might be or for leverage to appeal for help from state politicians to aid us in our peculiar situation.

We tried hiring another attorney who would listen to us first before listening to the "opposition". That did not happen. Attorneys seem to listen to police to see where the case stood and what direction they should go. Which sounds logical; however, we always ended up at the low end of the totem pole. We seemed to have no voice or seemed that we were the scourge of the earth parents.

A talk show called because they wanted to do a show on missing persons. A time was tentatively setup to meet in New York City. They called back later the same day to say they couldn't get things together. They would try to get back with us later that same year. We did not hear from them again.

Unsolved Mysteries called with an eleven-minute script to be aired on December 1, 1995. He read the script to Bob and Bob jotted down what he said:

Opening Scene: Video of Aaron and Bonnie opening presents.

Narrator: Christmas of 1992 was a happy time for Bonnie and her son Aaron. Less than two weeks later, she was reported missing. The police suspect her husband is responsible.

A surprise witness was Aaron Haim who implicated his father.

The family is in dispute over Bonnies disappearance.

Cut to Annie Harmon: "Bonnie would not run away. She loved her son too much."

Cut to Bob Pasciuto: "Thousands of women leave their families every year."

Narrator: Michael was the manager of a construction supply company and Bonnie was a accountant there.

Annie Harmon: "Mike was verbally abusive to Bonnie at work and at least once was physically abusive. Bonnie had decided to leave Michael."

Narrator: Bonnie opened a savings account using work address and Michael found out about it. An argument followed. Bonnie gave money to a friend to hold. Bonnie placed a deposit for an apartment and enrolled Aaron in a new school.

Annie Harmon: On January 6th, Bonnie was supposed to come to my house, but she called and cancelled her plans. The next day neither Bonnie or Michael showed up for work."

Narrator: Her purse was found buried in a dumpster.

Hickel: "Robbery does not appear to be the motive since her purse contained cash and credit cards."

Annie Harmon: "When I arrived at the Red Roof Inn, Michael did not have much to say."

Narrator: Neither Michael or his attorney would make a public statement other than Michael was innocent.

Hickel: "Michael said he called his mother about 3 am. His mother said Michael drove around looking for Bonnie about 45 minutes."

Narrator: Detective Hickel was not convinced this was routine. His instincts lead him to find Bonnies car parked at the airport parking lot. The seat was pushed back farther than it would have been if Bonnie had left it, and the floor mat showed a pristine foot print with a distinctive tread pattern unique to a limited-edition shoe.

Bob Pasciuto: The shoe print is interesting, but my shoe prints are probably in my wife's car. That doesn't really prove anything.

Narrator: In a bold move, police had a child psychologist interview Aaron. Aaron told the psychologist that he witnessed his father kill his mother.

Bob Pasciuto: "A child's credibility must be put in prospective. Aaron is also supposed to have said that his mother's car is at the bottom of a lake.

Jim Kow: "Children don't lie."

Narrator: Aaron's custody Is still in litigation; however, Aaron is safe. The family is split over this tragedy.

Bob Pasciuto: "There is still no proof of what happened."

Annie Harmon: "Michael is guilty of murder."

Bob Pasciuto: "We will not give up hope of finding Bonnie until we see proof."

Robert Stack: "Michael Harmon has not been arrested. The police still consider him to be a suspect and believe he may have had an accomplice in dropping off the car. It is possible that Bonnie Harmon is still alive. She is a petite 5'3 and wears her brown hair short.

Anyone with information should contact the city sheriff's office or Unsolved m Mysteries.

Bob told them that publicly using Aaron's name in the manner they scripted especially about the custody litigation was against the gag order in this case. They said that the State Attorney for this case, Jim Kow, said the wording complied with the gag order since it is public knowledge that a custody case is being held. We were concerned about preventing embarrassment and psychological trauma to Aaron. His schoolmates, parents, teachers, etc. who watch the show may very well ask him questions at school, church, playground, or other uncontrolled environments.

Bob asked for a letter be sent to *Unsolved Mysteries* asking them not to use Aaron's name. Bob also stated that since we have no control over Aaron's environment, that Aaron's therapist, Laura Creeper, should be allowed to preview the segment to prepare Aaron and his foster parents. The court should also be notified that we are concerned and ask the court to determine if the gag order is being violated and hear Laura Creeper's opinion on whether Aaron should be allowed to watch the show.

Bob stated that he realized that TV shows like to have shows that are compelling and controversial. He had no problem with the controversial part to help publicize Bonnie's disappearance, but did have a problem with the pity over Aaron to be the compelling part.

To our knowledge, the show never aired.

It is amazing that Annie Harmon seems to be a main character when she really knew Bonnie less than five years and that last year Bonnie was actually trying to get away from Berry and Annie Harmon. As far as the apartment lease, Bonnie picked up the deposit the next day proving she was not serious about finding an apartment. She did not have a new school for Aaron in Orange Park.

Bonnie wasn't really reported missing. It was less than twelve hours since she left her home and her purse was found not buried but on the top of the dumpster pile that was close to the airport with all the contents inside. That should have been a tip to check out motels, airlines, and the airport parking lots. If they did check the airport parking lot and her car was not there then and it later was, who put it there? It obviously was not Mike nor his parents because they were either at the police station, lawyer's office or being watched by the police department. If several people told police they saw Bonnie in the same area, it stands to reason that they did indeed see Bonnie the morning of January 7th.

The bold move to question a three-year-old for seven hours where I was present for much of the time seems deplorable to me. A taping of that interview would show that Aaron was not stating that he saw his father kill his mother but instead was playing with toys stating what happened during different recent times with his mom and dad or someone else. The police found no evidence to substantiate what Aaron stated as solid evidence that Aaron was a witness to the murder of his mother.

It has been stated several times during this time, that our family was in dispute over what happened to Bonnie. We have always been a loving family and nothing has changed since Bonnie's disappeared. We are each willing to help one another even though our opinions differ on the disappearance of Bonnie.

We do not know or understand why the police have been so deceptive of so many details about Bonnie's disappearance. It is difficult to understand why some of the puzzle pieces haven't shown what really happened the last few months of Bonnie's life before she disappeared.

Chapter Sixteen
No Justice for Bonnie

On September 18, 1995, a licensed psychologist gave Stephanie Lane an HRS foster care counselor a report on Michael Harmon. The report stated that the psychologist could see no reason why Michael should not have visitation rights reinstated and be reunited with Aaron. Then on November 2, 1995, a Judicial Review Hearing, the goal was for reunification. On December 6,1995, an order on foster care took place. It stated that the factual findings were:

1. That the child was previously adjudicated dependent and placed in the temporary care, custody of the Department of Health and Rehabilitative Services for appropriate foster care placement.
2. That the Department has made reasonable efforts to avoid or eliminate the necessity for the removal of the child from his home, and since his removal has diligently pursued reunification of the family, and
3. That it would be contrary to the best interests of the child to return him to his home or family at this time, and that there are clear and compelling reasons not to do so.

Aaron was to remain in foster care, and his therapy continued. The next review was scheduled for April 18, 1996. This was rescheduled for April 23, 1996.

While the hearings were going on for visitation rights and reunification, Michael was the plaintiff against Berry, Annie and Harmon's Tool and Fastener for his portion of the business. The final judgment came January 9, 1996. Michael was granted 15% of the business. According to Berry the business was worth four million dollars which meant Michael was entitled to $600,000. I do not know if he ever saw one penny of that amount.

On the 25th of January 1996, Michael's attorney wanted to file an appeal but needed to know whether the judge wanted the appeals to proceed on the basis of the trial court's approved stating and concluding with the orders being sealed. With that, Mr. Fallen initiated the appeal, only to be told, it wasn't good enough. The page numbers were not referenced on the issues presented, there was inappropriate type more than ten characters per inch, and the brief would not lie flat when it was opened. That took place until June 1997 when the appeal was denied. Ultimately, Michael lost his parental rights.

Michael had a girl friend for the last couple years. The police said she was wearing Bonnie's clothes. It was a little upsetting but it had been a long couple of years, and he needed someone. They never married. Michael's mom and dad moved to Tennessee. Michael decided to go with them after Michael was harassed by a neighbor and he had a difficult time finding a good job. Carolyn and John's youngest daughter stayed in their old house until a number of year years later. Michael and Bonnie's house now belonged to Aaron.

On January 12, 1996, a segment on *Unsolved Mysteries*, it stated that Bonnie came home from work at 7:30. She was supposed to be at Annie's at 8:00. I did not think this through before. Why would Bonnie go to Wal Mart, then to see her friend if she had an appointment to be at Annie's at 8:00? It takes a half-hour to get there from Bonnie's house. She had to take Aaron home, feed him, and put him to bed (his bedtime was 8:00). This did not seem to be wise planning on Bonnie's part which was unlike Bonnie. Perhaps, she really did not want to meet with Annie.

I decided to go back to school. It started to be part time so I could continue to work; however, my principal encouraged me to stop working and go full time to school. I wasn't young any longer. Bob was gone much of the time and our youngest child was now going into middle school. It wasn't easy, but we all managed to survive. I still wrote letters and tried to find someone who was interested in the case. I never succeeded in those areas. I did succeed in getting my degree in special education. I went on to receive my Master's Degree in Education. I taught at the elementary school level until I retired.

In January 2000, a new TV show called Hitting Home wanted to do a segment on Bonnie's disappearance. The show never aired, but it was in the newspaper. Any coverage was good. I had wished it would have developed into new information that would help find out what happened to Bonnie.

I received a letter in 2007 stating that since Bonnie was now declared deceased, I was the beneficiary of her Profit-Sharing Plan in Harmon's Tool & Fastener Services, Inc would I relinquish my rights to those interests. The interests were supposedly to go to Aaron. I did not have a lawyer to tell me what the formalities were concerning this matter. I still was not convinced Bonnie was even dead. I received four more letters that all I needed to do was sign my name on the signature line. I did not know if I did not respond to the letters, I relinquished my rights. How much the interests were, I do not know. I did find out that the money did go to Aaron.

In 2008, I asked the cold case unit if we could have a reinvestigation. I was told at that time that it was not a cold case. I just could not find a way to find justice for Bonnie no matter what I tried. Of course, with five other children there was plenty to keep me busy plus 18 grandchildren. There were disappointments and blessings all the time.

One of the blessings that has kept me busy is that my daughter Veronica bought a farm that she calls Celestial Farms. The whole family has come together to help her clean-up and fix-up the farm. Many volunteers have also helped to make it a great place for children and families. It is an animal rescue shelter that rescues farm animals not dogs or cats. I usually worked on the farm on Saturday unless I had a project I was working on and I would come after school on some days. It kept me busy as the garden manager. When I retired, I've spent six days helping out at the farm.

When 2013 came around, I called the cold case unit again. This time I was told it was a cold case, but in order for me to open it up, I would have to have new information to begin the investigation. Again, I could not get my foot in the door. It did not seem that all the old information was investigated thoroughly.

A surprising turn of events happened in December 2014. Aaron was removing the pool at his old home where Bonnie disappeared when a part of a skull came in view. The police were called and the State Attorney came out to look at what was found. An autopsy took place, but the police decided to send a tooth to Texas to have an analysis done to verify that the tooth was Bonnie's. It took a year for the skull and tooth to be verified as that of Bonnie's.

We were definitely surprised and did not know what to think or believe. We could not believe it could be Bonnie's body because the property had been searched inside and out several times with nothing being discovered. Bob was present during one of the searches and searched outside without the police present and could not find anything disturbed to indicate a newly dug area.

An update for *Unsolved Mysteries* stated that Aaron told psychologists that his father threw a shotgun out of the car shortly after he killed his mother. He told his foster mother the specific bridge. The police did find a shotgun. That gun belonged to his foster brother. Mike's guns were recorded on police records. A tip that the police followed up on but not a written statement written by an adult stating where Bonnie's body could be found!?

Different news stories during the next few years mention that just a skull was found and that Aaron was a witness to his father killing his mother. That is poor reporting and police investigation. It really has never been proven that Aaron saw anything. Even today, he does not remember anything. So, how can he be a prime witness?

In 2015, we had a yard sale to raise money for the feeding and care of the animals at Celestial Farms. A mother and her daughter came to the yard sale. The first thing the daughter did was to strike up a conversation about Bonnie. She said she was Michaels old girl friend that was now married with three children. She went on to say that Michael was good to her and her mother, that he was not abusive to her, and never said anything about doing harm to Bonnie. One of the last statements she made was that Amie Harmon was only trying to help Bonnie. I am afraid I blew it then. I told her I did not have the same feelings. I felt Annie must have asked her to have this conversation to find out my feelings. How else would she have known Annie and what Annie was trying to do?

Eight months later while I was at school teaching, I received a message that my husband called. When I called him to see what was up, he told me the results of the Texas autopsy came back that it was Bonnie's tooth. I asked for permission to go home and was immediately given permission. My husband said a police officer came by to give him the news. At least, we did not have to hear it first on the news. I was upset and when I am upset, I like to work. I went outside and started to work in the backyard. My husband came out to tell me our daughter Liz came over to talk to us. I was still too upset to talk to anyone. I was still going over it all in my mind.

Fifteen to thirty minutes later, I went in the house. Liz and Bob were sitting at the dining room table. I sat quiet and listened to them talk. I had already decided that we were missing the whole story. Liz then brought up the question of what to do with the body whether we wanted the remains as small as they were to be cremated. I then was quick to tell her as the parents, we would make that decision when the trial was over. I know she must have felt uncomfortable, and I didn't want to be mean hearted, but I felt the police or someone in control had asked her to ask us about disposing of the body. That was pretty much the end of Liz's meeting. It wasn't family members getting together to console one another.

Bob had many mixed feelings. We both felt Michael knew more than what he told us or anyone; however, we did not feel he murdered Bonnie. Bob was taking this all harder because he could not do anything to help Bonnie or any part of the situation to find out what had happened to Bonnie. The Harmon's were told not to contact us in any way. I decided it would not be wise to contact them.

I decided it would be a good time to find an attorney to rock the boat and sue the police and the State Attorney's Office. I went to the offices of some attorneys and was told they did not do that kind of work. I went on-line to learn more. I was told what type of attorney I needed and could not find one in our large city. I was down but did not feel out.

January 2018, I called Tom Fallen's office to see if he could meet me at Celestial Farms. We set a date that was really raining and muddy at the farm. I brought Bob's binders that were filled with day to day notes from the beginning of 1993 until we lost all hope of custody of Aaron. The meeting went well with both of us receiving information. I received information that I did not know before and Mr. Fallen received information that he forgot after twenty years or the police did not give to him.

Mr. Fallen informed me that the whole skeletal remains were uncovered with two items of clothing. One item was a Disney poncho that she didn't have at the time of her disappearance. No jewelry was found and no shoes or bra. I also was told that Berry Harmon's finger prints were found in Bonnie's glove compartment in her car. Another piece of information that really upset me was that a letter the police obtained in the spring of 1996 stating that Bonnie was buried where her body was eventually found in 2014.

If the police had investigated the credibility of the letter, we would know more about how and when Bonnie died. It would have been easier to determine that it was indeed Bonnie. It would have given us a better chance to have been closer to Aaron. While they were waiting for Aaron to give them information and looking her in lakes, rivers, and under bodies that were buried the same time Bonnie disappeared, they should have used information that was credible and easy to substantiate not a small child who could not determine time frame or who he saw throw a gun in the water.

I could not understand why the police were so deceptive about finding a whole skeleton. Everyone assumed it was just part of a skull and a tooth that had been found. I was so confused about "them" wanting to know about cremating the body so soon before the case went to trial and finding more than a skull. I wanted the autopsy report that was done in our city. Mr. Fallen stated that he and the Harmon's were sure it was Bonnie's body, so, why the deception?

The 29th of March 2018, Bob and I were invited to meet in the State Attorney's Office to discuss the case. That was a first! Aaron, Liz, Aaron's foster mother, her daughter, Annie, Berry, Bob and I all met in a conference room. After all the preliminary business of names, addresses, evidence to take the case to court. Supposedly, Michael had told two inmates while he was in jail before bail was set that he killed Bonnie. Of course, now they were out of jail and they could not depend on their testimony's. In other words, the inmates' statements were made as part of a plea bargain.

I realized more and more that I needed to do something to motivate finding out what happened to Bonnie. I wanted justice! The first item on my agenda was to find out more information about the place Bonnie spent much of her time the last few months before she disappeared. That was setting up a new place of business for Harmon's Tool and Fastener. That shop was on a main highway into Granville.

When we were going back and forth to the Granville Hospital with my mother in 2013, I noticed a very worn sign that stated that Harmon's Tool & Fastener was up for sale. I thought it was odd that a business would be up for sale for such a long time. Bob and I decided to take a trip to Granville in March of 2018. There was no for sale sign, and the store said open for business. The first part of the store was vacant and looked as though it had been vacant for a long time. The rest of the small shopping stores looked just as dingy, however, the door said open Monday-Friday from 9:00-5:00. Closed on Saturday and Sunday. The last door was blocked by shelving or some other item. There was an office set-up in the middle portion and what looked to be shelving in the last portion but did not look like a real inventory. The back of the building looked to be more like a car repair shop rather than a place to park work trucks or for material to be unloaded. None of the vehicles had Harmon logo on them. I knew the building had more issues than met the eye. It was supposed to be a five-star business according to the online information.

In August, I decided to hire a private investigator to find out about Harmon's Tool and Fastener business in Granville. That was the last place Bonnie worked at to start up a new Harmon's Tool and Fastener store that the police never questioned the Harmon's about or had searched. The building that seemed to be unnoticed and undisturbed since Bonnie was at that site. I felt strongly that it might contain answers to Bonnies disappearance.

I did some researching. Decided on an investigating service. The response to one was difficult to make contact and gain an appointment to meet and discuss what I wanted investigated. I decided to go with my second choice and prayed it would be the right one. We met, things seemed to go smoothly. I told Jimmy exactly what I wanted him to do to have it completed quickly. Then, I didn't hear from him for a few weeks and decided to email him. Jimmy answered promptly by saying he was working on different scenarios. I immediately emailed him back stating that that was not what I hired him to do and said that if he could not do the job, I hired him to do or I would find someone who would. He emailed back that he would do the job.

He emailed me a week later asking if I knew about a neighbor who had arguments with Michael after Bonnie disappeared. At first, I said no, then, I remembered that Michael had difficulties with a neighbor who was very obnoxious. Michael had had it with the harassment and decided to move to another state with his parents. I began to feel I made the wrong choice. I felt that it should only have taken him a week or two at the most to find out the information I hired him to investigate.

There was another delay in the trial process. On October 30, my husband and I decided to make another trip to Graineysville to see what we could find out to obtain information for ourselves. I was greatly surprised at what we saw. It was a hundred- and eighty-degree change. The building no longer had a flat roof line. Instead of the flat roof line, it had a dark brown façade that looked like an old general store type building with Harmon's Tool and Fastener name in huge letters. The windows were gleaming with drapes hanging on the sides of each window. The middle portion of the building had a decorative diamond design in silver. There was one truck in the parking lot with Harmon's logo on its door and another car. On the left side of the building separated by a driveway was a used car lot that seemed to extend beyond and behind Berry's business. It now appeared to be a three- or four-star business all in a relatively short period of time. Twenty-five and a half years later and right after we decided to have it investigated.

There just seemed to be too many coincidences throughout the last 25 years to all be coincidences. There was nothing that could be done to change the past. I just wanted to cry, scream, or something, but what would that accomplish?

It has been reported on the television news stations that 83% of the crimes in our city are unsolved. It was probably a lot less in 1993; however, it does not say too much for their investigative techniques.

The trial date has been changed so many times the past three years. The last two dates have been from illness and surgery for Michael's lawyer. It is now set February 5, 2019. The judge stated there would be no more motions to prolong the trial. More than 26 years after Bonnie first disappeared. Five years after Michael was arrested. Countless dollars on everyone's part to lead us to what? Sources from the State Attorney's Office mentioned that it may lead to a mistrial. This would satisfy no one and answers none of our questions. We are back to square one because a thorough investigation was never completed from day one. This has caused the murder of Bonnie, many heartaches, disgust, disbelief in the system, the loss of time and joy with our grandson and other children Bonnie may have had. It has also been a large part of my husband's health problems. Have we reached the end for justice for Bonnie? It appears so.

Bonnie was a giving person. She was not a taker or someone who did not care. Her siblings have been the same. They have always helped those around them. They have all sought ways to help solve this case or be a genuine help to family members. It is sad to feel that the system has sought ways to tear the family apart to gain their own agenda to solve the disappearance and murder of Bonnie making Mike the murderer.

I certainly feel we deserve to have our questions answered. The police could answer many of our questions. The answers would show that Michael was not the prime suspect in Bonnie's disappearance and that Bonnie's death was not on January 6, 1993; however, the where, how, and when she died cannot be established now since the police missed that chance in 1996 when they received a letter stating where her body was buried. We have not been told whose DNA was found on the envelope of the letter stating where her body was buried or whether that has been deemed undetermined. It seems since they do not have any evidence against Michael, they have no case and no recourse but to declare it a mistrial. Again, No Justice for Bonnie or for any of the family members.

Do I feel God has deserted me? No. I know that those guilty of wrongs will receive their justice now or when God chooses. Eternity is a long, long time.

About the Author

Patty is the mother of six children. Bonnie was the third child but the second pregnancy. Patty had twins the first pregnancy. Her husband was in the Navy, then, retired to also travel in engineering consulting work. She was a stay at home mom that volunteered at her children's schools. Much of the time, she was the only parent present to raise the children; however, her husband was very much an important figure in the children's lives. The children saw different parts of the United States and some other areas of the world, they were well educated and loved to read. Later in life, Patty became a special education teacher with a master's degree in education. This book, No Justice for Bonnie, is a way to tell her side of the story about Bonnie, her disappearance, and the injustice that transpired from her disappearance.

www.ingramcontent.com/pod-product-compliance
Lightning Source LLC
Chambersburg PA
CBHW021434210526
45463CB00002B/512